50p

THE ORCHESTRA SPEAKS

THE AUTHOR playing in the B.B.C. Symphony Orchestra

TOSCANINI

THE ORCHESTRA
SPEAKS

BY

BERNARD SHORE

PRINCIPAL VIOLA B.B.C. SYMPHONY ORCHESTRA

With a Frontispiece

LONGMANS, GREEN AND CO.
LONDON ❖ NEW YORK ❖ TORONTO

LONGMANS, GREEN AND CO. LTD.
OF PATERNOSTER ROW

43 ALBERT DRIVE, LONDON, S.W.19
NICOL ROAD, BOMBAY
17 CHITTARANJAN AVENUE, CALCUTTA
36A MOUNT ROAD, MADRAS

LONGMANS, GREEN AND CO.
55 FIFTH AVENUE, NEW YORK, 3

LONGMANS, GREEN AND CO.
215 VICTORIA STREET, TORONTO, I

First published - - - - 1938
New Impression   July 1938
New Impression   - August 1938
New Impression November 1938
New Impression December 1938
New Impression November 1939
Reprinted by Novographic
Process March 1941 March 1942,
September 1942,   January 1943,
May 1943,   December 1944
and   January 1946.

CODE NUMBER: 14411

PRINTED IN GREAT BRITAIN BY
LOWE AND BRYDONE PRINTERS LIMITED, LONDON, N.W.10

DEDICATED TO

RICHARD CAPELL

CONTENTS

ACKNOWLEDGMENT

The photographs of the Author and of Toscanini, appearing as the frontispiece, are supplied by the B.B.C. and the Exclusive News Agency respectively.

PRELUDE

PRELUDE

THE Scene: Queen's Hall; the time, 8.10 p.m. The orchestra assembles. A symphony concert is to be directed by a famous conductor.

The house is filling, although there will at 8.15 still be the few empty seats of those inevitable late-comers who never permit themselves to hear an overture.

As the players take their seats the state of the house is generally remarked upon.

"That's better! A packed house at last! A difference from last week, when it was papered from top to bottom. And then they didn't come, but sent their servants!"

In the few precious minutes before the arrival of the leader the orchestra is occupied with final preparations. Chairs are shuffled about, and one wonders why there is less room on the platform than there was in the morning. The string players move their arms about far more than if they were actually playing, to ensure ample space for a climax. Inside players—those seated on the left of each desk —turn up the corners of the music. Leaders perhaps give a last look at a tricky solo passage, hoping that it will come off better than the other day. Each leader, string or wind, has with him a second principal who is responsible for turning over the music and for help in every way—a moral support. This "plumber's mate" role of the second principal is of the utmost importance. It either lightens the prin-

3

cipal's work and responsibility or makes life a burden. A rare friendship may spring up between No. 1 and No. 2 of a department. Lucky the leader who has a friendly lieutenant, not out to compete but to back him up and help in the job.

The first violins, called upon for more virtuosity as a rule than the other strings, give a last-minute look at an awkward passage or two; *sotto voce*, or, while going over one's strings for tuning, one surveys the audience. A player nudges a neighbour.

"There's Epstein!"

"Where's he sitting?"

"Do you see that fellow with a bald head and side-whiskers turning his back to us and talking to a girl with red hair—half-way down the stalls in the centre? Well, just behind him, in a line with us, there's a woman with an ear-trumpet. Epstein's sitting in the same row, about six seats to the left."

A player mutters to himself.

"I've tried sixteen blessed fingerings and none of them come off." (Turns to his partner.) "Harry, how do you finger this infernal passage?"

"1st on E, 4th on G sharp, and pray for luck on the top B. It comes off, sometimes!"

The second violins on the other side, with less interesting and exacting parts to play, will be rather more carefree. Not that the principal second violin is without his particular share of responsibility, since conductors have a way of turning their backs on his department for the sake of the beloved firsts, and the most tricky entries may have to be made sure of by the leader of the seconds.

The violas, the serious department, shuffle about with chairs to claim adequate room for their heavy and arm-aching instruments.

Message from the back: "Can you give us an inch? They say they've got no room."

"No, neither have we."

No. 1 to himself, after a fruitless search in every pocket: "No mute!" Then to the desk behind: "Send down to Arthur and ask him to be a good fellow and lend me one."

No. 3 grumbles: "What does he do with his mutes? I've lent him six already. His room must be full of them. Why doesn't he collect something sensible?"

No. 6: "Have those two in front made up their great minds about the bowing at No. 41 in the symphony? Pass it along. Is it down or up?"

Indignant reply! "Down, of course!"

"Well, you played it up this morning!"

The 'cellos, an irresponsible, cheerful lot, have begun operations by digging themselves good and hearty into the platform with their spikes. A 'cellist must have a sense of humour, seeing that he has to spend most of his waking hours leaning over a long box.

It is curious, the correspondence between the instruments and the temperament of their players. The violinist is of a feminine and capricious disposition, full of brilliance and exuberant spirit, with a wonderful capacity for rushing about here and there. The violist is generally reflective, with a touch of melancholy about him. The 'cello department of any orchestra provides more humour and cheerful spirits than all the other members of the family put together, and none make such a cacophony when tuning. The effect of the continual tuning of 'cellos is possibly the reason for the pensiveness of their next of kin.

No. 1 picks up his 'cello, looks inside at the soundpost; decides that the twenty-third position he tried last night was probably the best, and plans to find it again when he gets home.

At the last minute he turns to instruct the department not to start a competitive race in the scherzo, such as had occurred that morning.

The basses are the most spectacular in their preparations, and almost blatant in spit and polish and the general grooming of their charges. Tuning amongst the basses— or dog-houses, as they are sometimes known—is always a little suggestive of the stables, though the conversation of the players may range from masonry to poetry.

There is always a good-humoured war between basses and 'cellos, each affecting a slight contempt of the other.

"You 'cellos think that because a passage is easy for your rotten instrument, it is the same for us. We want a lot of bow for that phrase."

"All right," say the 'cellos, "do it your own way, if you must play on a thing that no dog would like to use."

There is a legend that this ancient feud began at the Opera many years ago, in the days when the principal bass and principal 'cello shared a desk. On account of the size of the larger instrument, there was a tradition that the 'cellist should turn over. For years the two lived amicably together, but a day came when a new 'cellist, who fancied himself, declared that he and his whole race had stood this indignity long enough and no more would a 'cellist serve a mere bass player. The bass player asserted by way of retort that the loss of his immortal soul was to be preferred to sharing a desk with such an upstart. Since that day they have never lived together, and indeed the two departments are now mostly to be seen at opposite sides of the orchestra.

In these days the banter exchanged is good-natured unless the two departments, sharing a tune, are pulled up for bad intonation. Then each scowls at the other. But only if the principal 'cellist is unwise enough to suggest that it matters little where the basses put their left hands, since they never get within six inches of the proper note, do basses become dangerous.

A Toscanini story—remember that Toscanini was once a 'cellist—illustrates this rivalry. He was reprimanding the bass soloist at his entry in the Ninth Symphony for singing his note-values too precisely.

"Why do you sing so correct? It must be *rubato, rubato, rubato*. Sing it freely! Who told you to sing it so correct?"

"Well, Maestro, as a matter of fact it was X." And a distinguished conductor was named.

"Oh," exclaimed Toscanini scornfully, "der bass player!"

Among the woodwind, reeds are the burning question. While the instruments are being warmed reeds are carefully tested—and some are found wanting.

Clarinets are busy with their brace of instruments each. Both No. 1 and No. 2 play scales up and down, pianissimo, and a squeak worries No. 1.

"There you are, Winkle, that's the fourth reed I've tried to-day."

Winkle opens his box and hands him one of his own.

"Try this one, Jack. How's that?"

"Fine! You're a true friend, boy."

Flutes and brass have no reed worries and can snatch a moment's rest before the curtain. Third trombone informs his neighbour that he's just finished making his fourth viola, and has just put on the twenty-fifth coat of varnish. Two of his instruments are in the orchestra.

The tuba player, sheltering behind his instrument, remarks to the bass trombone:

"I should like a pound for every quart of air I've pumped into this radiator, just warming it up. I'm exhausted before the concert." Lugubrious mutter: "What a life!"

That heartfelt sigh is at some time or another echoed by every member of the orchestra. As a vocation, orchestral playing cannot satisfy the craving for freedom and self-expression latent in the musician's heart. Some excellent players will have none of it, and prefer to play unaccompanied Bach outside Queen's Hall. They are able, at least, to hear their own performances, when and where they choose, while their brothers in the orchestra may not have heard themselves play for years. Moreover, we have to make music when and where we are told!

If the young orchestral player realized what his life would become he would scarcely start on his career with delight and exuberance. "What a life!" Rehearsal from 10 a.m. to 1 p.m. six days a week, for eleven months of the year, whatever the time of the concert the night before. Then perhaps another rehearsal from 2.30 until 5.30. The evening may be free, but if the player is preparing for a concerto or chamber concert that must be used for practising, rehearsing or possibly teaching. A leader, who is always faced with great competition, is in danger of losing his place unless he continually keeps himself in form and able to do anything required of him.

Chamber music keeps a man musically alive as much as anything, but if a quartet means business the four players will spend their entire free time rehearsing. It is no easy matter to combine chamber music with full-time orchestral work. It means this kind of thing:

Orchestra rehearsal	10.0–1.0 p.m.
Orchestra rehearsal	2.30–5.30 p.m.
Quartet rehearsal, run through	6.30–7.30 p.m.
Chamber concert	8.30–10.30 p.m.

Promenade concerts, it has been maintained, mean "the easiest time for the orchestra."

"What more do they want?" said a conductor. "The orchestra is free from 1 p.m. until 8 p.m."

But two journeys up to town and back mean three hours out of the day gone bang! Orchestra players cannot afford to live near their work. These long evenings involve a great strain, especially for all the solo instruments in the wind, let alone the strings. The exhaustion experienced after a Promenade concert—the first half is in itself a complete symphony concert—becomes nearly intolerable as the weeks go on.

Many an amateur in the audience thinks how exciting and

9

delightful an orchestral player's life must be. This is an illusion. The life is one of incessant strain and back-breaking work in which minutes of pleasure are paid for by hours and hours of slogging. As for chamber music, the pecuniary reward works out at $2\frac{1}{2}d.$ or $3d.$ an hour, for the first four or five years. After that rather more, when a repertory has been built up.

A stale and slow-moving mind is of no use in a first-class orchestra, and an unfit body cannot cope with the physical strain involved. Those players really worth their salt are frequently expert at other accomplishments. In a single department there may to-day be found a cartoonist who can turn out as subtle a caricature as many a professional artist; a mechanic who can compete with any expert model-maker and, incidentally, put his hand to anything that requires great technical skill and thought. The leader himself is a scientific horticulturist and an artist in photography. These talents are in one department of 'cellos. It is generally found that the finer the artist, the more versatile he is.

The orchestra seen in full war-paint a minute or two before the concert gives the impression of great things to come, with everyone keyed up to concert pitch. How has the required pitch been reached? The greater part of the con-ductor's work has already been done at rehearsals. The concert is but another rehearsal, without stopping or inter-ruption. These rehearsals may have been carried through calmly; or the orchestra, in spite of looking keyed up, may be wilting from experiences endured in the morning.

Strange things may have happened before the orchestra assembles for the concert. Once, at a final rehearsal, a very large conductor showed no sign of stopping at 1 p.m. (Morning rehearsals in this country are nearly always from 10 a.m. to 1 p.m.) Double-basses were being rubbed down to remind him that the time had expired; still he went on. About 1.10 p.m. the first horn emptied his instrument and went off. In a trice the conductor was after him, trumpeting like an angry elephant. The horn player then took his coat off and asked him if he wanted a fight. But the leader of the orchestra—a brave man—had followed in the wake of the conductor, and with one or two more friends stepped between them and called off both the fight and the rehearsal.

Pouring oil on troubled waters is an important part of the leader's job. He is the liaison officer between orchestra and conductor. If the conductor is overwrought the leader is there to calm him. If he gets lost, the leader brings him into touch again with the orchestra. If the orchestra is perplexed as to the meaning of a beat, a tactful suggestion from the leader may make it clear.

Members of the public often misconceive the leader's role. One has heard it said:

"Surely the orchestra is supposed to watch the stick? What has the leader to do with it?"

The leader has a great deal to do with it. The attack of the whole orchestra, and particularly that of the strings, has to be led by him. It is a psychological matter. He has, without any enormous gesture, to make himself felt. The maintaining of the conductor's grip is partly his responsibility too. Most of this side of his work naturally lies in his own department, the first violins—the most vital section of the orchestra. Nevertheless, a leader with great vitality and strength of personality can communicate this to the entire orchestra.

The result of a leader's influence may be warm-blooded and precise, or else cold and flabby, though the material be equally excellent in both cases. Counting bars is not the leader's only technical responsibility. Some of the rank and file do this. They enjoy finding the first desk wanting. The leader is primarily responsible for every entry.

When the conductor is good and wise, he works closely with his orchestral leader and always seeks his advice on technical matters. Woe to the conductor on bad terms with his leader! His work will be obstructed and he will obtain only a fraction of the orchestra's vitality and efficiency. The orchestra quickly perceives antipathy between the two, and this invariably has an adverse effect on its playing.

A good string leader can colour and grip a department, but it is the bad one whose tone stands out and is merely aggressive.

The leader of the orchestra is responsible for tuning, for the bowing directions, and all other technical matters for the strings. Not the least of his duties is looking after the general interests of the orchestra. We have known him to remind the conductor when to stop a rehearsal. One of the few causes of really serious trouble is a conductor's habitual over-time rehearsing.

In years gone by there was more excuse for this—in the days when two rehearsals only were fixed for symphony concerts; but nowadays, when rehearsals are adequate, there is no reason for it.

Foreigners, on the strength of our hatred of unduly prolonged rehearsals, have sometimes accused English orchestras of failing to enjoy music-making for music's sake. But in point of fact the only difference which a prolonged rehearsal makes in the effect at a concert is, as a rule, unnecessary strain and overtaxed vitality. Three hours is long enough for concentrated attention and playing. Conductors who feel consideration for their players and wish to get the last ounce out of them at the concert are wise not to use the full three hours on the morning of the concert.

For the players to get it into their heads that they are only rehearsing for the conductor's sake is fatal for effective and concentrated work. Whether it is necessary or not, some conductors will use every minute of the allocated time—demand their whole pound of flesh.

Fascinating though it may be to conduct a fine body of players, it is not always so enthralling to be conducted. The conductor has the pleasure of playing the autocrat, while not only must the player do what he is told, however much he disagrees, but he is continually being told to do contrary things—thus for one conductor he must play strong accents on both first and second beats of a bar in 2/4 time, and for another first beat strong and second weak. One conductor will want all solos "played out" strongly, with rich accompanying by the rest of the orchestra; another an exquisite *pp* accompaniment, and restrained solos. One conductor will tell the orchestra to pay scrupulous attention to everything set out in the parts; and the next one will rage and fume if the orchestra does not read between the lines.

The orchestra's work, then, is never done. The player's

fate is not to be steadily advancing towards ever finer performances, but constantly working with different minds—to be for ever doing and undoing. A certain Mozart symphony not long ago was more than adequately rehearsed under a conductor who insisted on purism. *Crescendi* and *diminuendi*, were extremely controlled, and only the barest expression marks were admitted. Shortly afterwards the same work was given under a temperamental conductor who demanded intense and warm-blooded playing. Practically every bar had to be unlearnt and then built up again in a totally different style.

To observe the different attitudes of mind in conductors is interesting, but there is something maddening in finding that a much-played work is never learnt for good and all. The chamber-music player knows what it is to have a certain repertory, which can be solidly learnt. The quartet can perpetually improve its work, but does not have to start all the technical business all over again, like the orchestra, for each performance. The orchestral classics have all to be rehearsed for hours and hours each time they appear on the programme, except in those favoured organizations with a permanent conductor.

The orchestra is in much the same position as a church congregation. The parson says what he likes: none may answer him back.

The orchestra is denied the conductor's joy of a full score; each player has only his own part before him, and soon knows its limitations, especially if he is an "inner part", that is, for instance, 2nd violin, 2nd viola, or 2nd wind. The fortunate 1st violins or the 1st wind instruments generally have interesting parts, and get a satisfaction and interest denied the less fortunate 2nd violins and violas, who in all the early classics find their parts a deadly bore. Little skill is required in playing them, save that of making dull parts interesting. In the inner parts of an early Haydn or Mozart symphony for anything like two or three bars of interesting music to play, one has three or four pages of reiterated quavers or endless sustained harmonies.

Modern scoring, however, from the days of Rimsky-Korsakov, has made orchestral playing a new art. Brahms, though he made all his part-writing interesting, kept within strict limits, but Strauss and Elgar went one better and gave the less-favoured members of the orchestra the joy of virtuoso parts to play.

For generations the 1st violins have been the spoilt darlings of the orchestra, and the 'cellos, though less spoilt, have usually had plenty of "fat"; but the violas and the 2nd violins of the early days of Haydn and Mozart, to say nothing of Bach and Handel, might have been members of the Plumbers' and Stonemasons' Guilds, and musicians only in their spare time, so seldom were they trusted out of shallow water.

Boredom is the greatest bugbear of orchestral playing. Nothing keeps it at bay like a really fine and difficult part to play. For those with no interesting parts on which to concentrate their minds and skill there is no ray of sunshine. Though the composition in hand may be beautiful as can be, it does not follow that they can hear it all. What a player hears of a score as a whole depends entirely upon his position. In a rising semi-circle one may hear almost as well as the conductor, but if the orchestra is on a level floor, then even those immediately beneath the conductor will only hear three-quarters of the sound properly.

The leader of the orchestra and his opposite number on the other side of the conductor have the best position. Even the middle of the favoured first semi-circle may be affected by an oboe in the vicinity, and it is surprising what a stinging noise that gentle instrument can make when its tone is pumped directly into one's ear. The players on the fringe of the orchestra, especially those behind the 1st violins, and on the other side, are worst off in this respect. They are cut off from the rest of the orchestra. They can hear their colleagues' slightest discrepancies, but everything else is indistinct. One may have the utmost difficulty in hearing a tune played softly by the woodwind, or by a remote department of the orchestra, and great concentration is necessary. But some conductors like all one's concentration to be given to them.

At Covent Garden if one is seated at one wing not a sound will be heard from the players at the other end, though far too much of one's neighbours. Though the following incident did not take place at Covent Garden, it illustrates the orchestral player's difficulty of hearing the essentials of a score. Two bass players in an opera company once expressed a wish to their conductor.

"Mr. G., we've played in this company for thirty years, and have never seen an opera from the front. Can you let one of us off to see 'Carmen' this afternoon?"

Mr. G. was delighted with the request and presented them with two tickets. But he could only let one go at a time. Having tossed up, No. 2 won, and took his wife with him. In the evening the conductor overheard the following conversation during the business of tuning:—

No. 1: "Well, George, how did you get on? What's the show like?"

No. 2: "Oh, grand! The girl taking Carmen looked a bit plump to my way of thinking. But she could sing—not half! And that there Toreador enjoys himself in his clothes. But Bert, what took me was something quite different. That Toreador, he's got a grand song to sing. You know, that number where we go

Well, there's a tune going on at the same time. Now we've never heard that, have we?"

Our two friends were playing, as usual, underneath the stage. In a symphony orchestra the basses are generally placed in a commanding position where they can hear most things. The wood-wind, high up in the centre of the orchestra, are also favoured, though they will get too much of the wind and too little 1st and 2nd violins. But for those placed in front of that formidable battery of brass, trombone and trumpets, the rest of the orchestra is apt to fade out when these come into action.

A conductor once told his orchestra: "One eye has to be on the music, the other on the conductor; one ear is for listening to the orchestra, the other for one's own performance!" If the mouth is, as it frequently may be, occupied with some dexterous work with a mute, the nose is really the only organ not in use.

It is practically impossible to listen intently to the faint warbling of a bass clarinet in its lowest regions, while one is engaged upon a passage that requires the entire resources of one's nervous system. However, adequate rehearsal makes the individual part familiar, and after a time the main foundations of the repertory become so much the player's second nature that it is a relief to detach one's thought from the individual part and allow the subconscious mind to deal with it. Listening then becomes easier and also sustains the interest. The larger the orchestra, the less detail one can hear, though this may be offset by the quality and mastery of the scoring.

Two outstanding works for a large orchestra, Holst's 'Planets' and Strauss's 'Zarathustra', both glorious to play, are very different from the listener's point of view inside the orchestra. Every detail of the 'Planets' stands out in stark relief, while Strauss's work is so intricate that quantities of detail are lost to the player, brilliant though the scoring is.

In Brahms's symphonies the orchestra depends enormously upon the conductor to hear clearly. The scoring demands one's unremitting attention to dynamics, and indeed it is essential to a clear performance that each player shall hear everything. The melodic line does not stand out by itself as in the later scoring of such composers as Rimsky-Korsakov and Elgar.

Choral concerts are hated by symphony orchestras. A large body of singers seems to deaden all one's own singing quality and makes intelligent listening a labour. If an organ is used as well, indispensable though it may be, one's own playing becomes quite inaudible, exhausting, and seems futile.

A choral concert involves implacably dull rehearsals. First the orchestra by itself—yards of sustained notes and intolerable dullness, mostly sheer accompaniment. Then, with the choir—we feel ourselves just fodder for the thing. After that, more fodder for the soloists. Lastly, the whole grand show, organ and everything else. There is generally only one final combined rehearsal, when the work is heard in its entirety for the first time, and the orchestral player has a good appetite if he is by then not too fed-up to listen. The story of the 'cellist who once dreamt he was playing in 'Messiah', and woke up to find he was, well describes the feelings of the artist doomed to play in a Handel oratorio with the original scoring.

A Bach concert at the Proms is another test of mental and physical endurance. 'Cellists have the worst time, especially the first desk or two. The lucky ones at the back only have to wake up now and then. Clarinettists revere Bach above all composers; on the other hand, oboes are sometimes overworked. In a certain Brandenburg concerto one can watch a relay race in progress: as one oboe gets pumped dry, another skilfully takes his place.

Sitting inside the orchestra at a Bach concert one often wonders, Why? When, after playing five Brandenburg concertos there is still one to go, a player thinks to himself: "Now, if I can stand up to this, I might have a chance in a six-day bicycle race."

The question has been asked whether, sitting in the

orchestra, one can form a useful opinion of a new work. The answer is that when one's position is good and there has been time to learn to play one's own part easily, by the last rehearsal one has a pretty good idea of what it is about. Concentrated listening is necessary, but if the scoring is good, the orchestra should be far more entitled to an opinion than any member of an audience hearing it for the first time.

The players' power of listening to one another varies with the acoustics of the hall.

When the whole orchestra sits in a great apse, the acoustics are probably good, but at Queen's Hall, where part of the strings are cut off from the rest of the orchestra by a great wall, then those players sitting below are unfortunate. The Albert Hall is, of course, a joke. Nothing can be heard save the echo. Sir Thomas Beecham was once rehearsing there when the hammering of some workmen caused him to exclaim:

"Splendid! They're pulling the damned place down at last!"

One of the finest halls for an orchestra's pleasure is the new Salle des Beaux-Arts at Brussels. There is room for the largest orchestra, and everything is heard to perfection.

Plenty of elbow room is a luxury the orchestral player has frequently to forgo. The string players in the centre are always huddled together, generally by force of encroachment on the part of the players at the edges. Then there is a flurry of bows and high language and the concertina is forced open again—to force them off the edge of the platform. A curious phenomenon is frequently observed at Queen's Hall. One might expect such an object as a grand pianoforte, placed in the centre of the platform, to cause discomfort to a large orchestra. But when this is removed, in the interval of a concert, there is none of the abounding vacant space that might have been hoped for. The aid of physical science should be called in to explain why the space no longer occupied by the piano is instantly filled again to suffocation, and there is less room than before. The wind players find themselves unable to raise their elbows. The only man who never complains is the timpanist—the reason, of course, is that he completely surrounds himself with his drums.

Another of the string player's troubles is his having to share a desk. How happy one could be with a desk to oneself as in a quartet! It is not comfortable for two to share—especially for short-sighted 'cellists and big violas. The violin is a small, handy instrument, and the violinists' difficulty is not so acute. But two large violas have to be managed, and never without some discomfort. It is amazing how few are the poked-out eyes or shattered peg-boxes.

Then personalities may clash. Some partners have not spoken for years. It is amusing for the wind when a scrap is in progress, for they get a good view and hope against hope for a spectacular finale with a smashed fiddle or two. But, the orchestra being in the main a patient animal, hearty rows seldom occur. It was an exceptional day when a fat fiddler was hoisted by the slack of his trousers and thrown down the stairs at the back of the Queen's Hall by an irritated viola player.

Accidents happen seldom in the orchestra nowadays; things are not what they were. The rare incidents at

Queen's Hall usually take the form of an interruption from the audience. Recently a gentleman suddenly rose to his feet in the balcony, after a performance of the Love Duet from 'The Valkyrie,' and shouted: "Less noise from the orchestra!" The effect he made was completely to disturb the atmosphere. The orchestra spent their spare time for the rest of the evening in trying to spot him on his next entry; but he did not perform again.

In the good old days this is the kind of thing that varied the monotony. At a large hall in the Midlands the orchestra platform was built up very high to accommodate chorus and orchestra, and on one occasion a more than usually large orchestra was being employed, with a corresponding lack of space. The kitchen department was crowded on the topmost tier and some of the heavy instruments had to be supported by blocks of wood and wedges. Everything was going well at the concert until sudden pressure on the percussion department necessitated a heavy whack on the bass drum with cymbals attached to it. It wobbled dangerously and the player, in a panic, hung on to it for life. That was too much for the supports: they slipped, and the whole concern, cymbals and all, but minus the player—who was hauled back by his friends to safety—started on a ponderous descent down the whole flight of the orchestra. The wood-wind barely cleared out of its way, leaving an A clarinet rather bent; but the violas at the bottom, having had plenty of warning, made a wide gangway and after the contraption, now at a good speed, had passed, they quietly went on with their work.

For years now we have waited in vain for the timpanist to

come unseated. All is efficient and serious now; no longer do the horns start off with Berlioz's Hungarian March when the rest of the orchestra are playing Boccherini's Minuet. This outrage was perpetrated once when the players were irritated by the management's economizing in programmes, and the Hungarian March happened to be the next piece on their stand.

Throughout a whole season of Proms there is no comic relief save the study of the faces of the public in the near proximity. Occasionally one appears that is worth watching, possibly for its beauty, or else for its violent emotional reactions to the music; more often there can be found one at least so vacant in expression that only the classic Kreisler story can do it justice. Walking with a friend one day he passed a large fish-shop where on the front slab, arranged in a row, lay a fine catch of codfish, with their mouths wide open and glassy eyes staring. Kreisler suddenly stopped, looked at them, and clutching his friend violently by the arm exclaimed:

"Heavens, they remind me—I should have been playing at a concert!"

Audiences make the same difference to the orchestra as to any artist. The players are naturally more on their mettle when the house is full, and a well-dressed one. It is more inspiring to see a background of beautiful colours than dingy ones. Since the orchestra has to be dressed in boiled shirts, it is refreshing for the players to see a corresponding courtesy on the part of the audience. Warm-hearted applause is also appreciated. It is depressing after a magnificent performance to find the audience cold and unmoved.

True, no one applauds the engine driver after a fast run, or a plumber after a finely wiped joint—why then should musicians be so spoilt? The answer is that we have to do all our work in public, with thousands of critical ears and eyes to carp and find fault.

The clerk in an office does not have to write a letter with a spotlight on him, surrounded by rubber-necked persons all concentrating on every mark of his pen. Musicians are not allowed to make a slip and rub it out.

There is enough nervous strain involved in the work itself to discourage friction between conductor and orchestra. When trouble arises it is generally smoothed over expeditiously.

A conductor sometimes looks at a player as though he had half a mind to descend from the rostrum and come to blows, but the threat remains in the air. In Beethoven's Ninth Symphony a Prussian conductor only went so far as to spit at an ambitious 4th horn player who had failed at the crucial moment.

Every conductor, whatever his eminence, is a component part of the orchestra. Like any other member, he can help in making an effect of a complete artistic whole or can produce an effect of ragged ends. His power in either direction is exceptional. The conductor can either interest and thrill the orchestra or make players wish they were dead.

The faces of orchestral players may often be studied with interest. Do they show alertness and sparkle, then there is a man in front of them; if no one appears to be interested in the stick or, in fact, in anything at all, then the conductor is unworthy.

When audiences and critics accuse orchestras of being slack and dull, the responsibility is largely the conductor's. Not that a second-rate orchestra can be made first-class by a fine conductor, though he may succeed in making it resemble one; but a magnificent orchestra will lose all its verve and perfection under the hands of a second-rate man.

Conductors have been known who were unable to start the orchestra without the help of the leader. Such was a clever business-man of music who once directed the music at a London theatre. It was a recognized thing that the leader of the band, Mr. S., should do all the real conducting necessary. Mr. S. was ill one night, and a deputy took his place. The conductor as usual raised his stick, and beyond gazing at the leader made no sign. Nothing happened: so with a pained look at the surprised leader, he put his stick down again. Then once more he raised it with added determination; the leader again put his bow on the strings ready for the down beat, which came not. At last the conductor, now thoroughly nettled, hissed:

"For heaven's sake, go on, man! What are you waiting for?"

Conductors have also been known who conducted a bar or two after the end of the piece. To a self-respecting orchestra the most trying are those who, incompetent musicians and conductors, yet talk and talk at the orchestra for the exquisite pleasure of hearing their own voices and of airing their shallow knowledge. When they are of mature years they are borne with fortitude and stoicism. But when they are young, their quackings lead almost to madness.

The orchestra is, in the main, a patient and loyal animal.

How often, from a common feeling of musicianship, has it pulled conductors through awkward situations!

In the band-room some disgruntled player occasionally threatens disaster to the concert.

"Look here, chaps, we've had enough of this fellow. Let's all follow the stick to-night and give him a lesson he won't forget!"

It is only a threat. The orchestra invariably saves the show.

Conductors under the age of thirty-five or forty are not popular with a first-class orchestra. For some reason the players resent being handled by a young man, and would rather have an experienced man of mature years than a youngster, no matter how brilliant. Above all, let the young conductor restrain a love of talking! It is not seemly for experts to listen to a young man airing his views of their playing. A fine player will not resent being criticized by a man who has proved his worth in the world, but it is another matter to be pulled up by a youngster who thinks he knows everything. Those who have the grace to wear a certain humility get on best. The greatest men, for that matter, have a certain humility about them. Toscanini is amazingly humble in his attitude to the composers he interprets.

"I am only a musician who always sings and tries to understand the music," he says. "It is so beautiful; and however many times I have played it I always study it afresh, as if I had not seen it before."

Contrast this with (from a youngster):—"This passage is always played wrong. I know it is generally played like that, but I'm going to show how it ought to be played!"

If the young man must be inflicted on experienced players, then let him at least be quiet, and bear in mind that he will do well if he "hardly upsets them" (as the Vienna Philharmonic said of a visiting conductor). Let him not make the wretched orchestra rehearse merely for his pleasure, but seek to get the best out of everyone by a quiet charm of manner, taking it for granted that all will do their best for him, if he is tactful, modest and able.

Some conductors get the worst out of an orchestra before a note is played. Their faces and whole demeanour seems to say:

"Now, you blackguards, I know you will let me down if you possibly can, but I'll just show you!"

After a few minutes there will probably be an explosion —he has detected a whisper, and of course with him as the subject! That is a curious characteristic of certain conductors; they think they are being whispered about, while in point of fact the matter of the whispering is always of something of importance—it may be a technical question, or else gardening or cross-words.

More conductors are spoilt by their faulty psychology than by musical incompetence. No matter what their knowledge of the scores or what their technique, or how complete even their knowledge of the capabilities of the orchestral instruments, if they ignore the human element in the players, they only succeed in bringing out the worst in them. Fine conductors not only show how good they are at their job but manage, too, to give the orchestra a sense of well-being. These artists, besides the confidence they inspire in themselves, give it to the orchestra as well.

They are not common, and are more than welcome to any orchestra that has had the experience of being talked at and over-corrected.

When conductors complain that they "cannot get anything out of the men—they are so slack and mulish"—the fault is more than likely in themselves. Either they rub the men up the wrong way, or they adore rehearsing. Half the battle is won if a conductor understands that an orchestra hates rehearsing for rehearsing's sake, but will do its best work if it knows that only when this is vitally necessary will it be called upon to go over passages or movements again and again. Toscanini is exemplary in this respect. He never plays a whole movement through merely for the sake of two or three doubtful passages. These passages will be put right, but, if satisfied, he does not rehearse the whole movement again "for luck".

The orchestra bears with composer-conductors. They are more individual and naturally they want to hear their work as much as possible. Beecham is one of the few conductors who can go on and on rehearsing and rehearsing. But Beecham is Beecham, and he can do what no one else on earth can attempt.

Another point frequently overlooked is this: when will foreign, and some English, conductors learn that an English orchestra must have something in reserve for the concert? It goes against the grain, against English temperament, to celebrate an occasion before the date. The question has nothing to do with slacking at rehearsal. Our players will give as much as any conductor need desire. But the night is something different from the morning of the day before.

An English orchestra will not look upon rehearsal as being other than a rehearsal. The concert is what matters. It is common sense to hold something in reserve for the night, and the players feel it reasonable for the conductor too to leave something in reserve.

SIR THOMAS BEECHAM

SIR THOMAS BEECHAM

WHEN Beecham was born some beneficent spirit entrusted with divine gifts for mortals must have had its attention suddenly distracted, and our friend ran off with the lot. How many are the unfortunates born at the same time, who have had to go short!

First is his rare gift of what, for want of a better name, I call his "inward vision," so apparent to all who have worked closely with him; and, what is rarer still, the ability to call upon it at will and express it illimitably in terms of music. Then his power of expressing himself to the orchestra is great enough to enable him to dispense with a conductor's technique. He possesses a prodigious memory, which never seems to fail him, and an extremely quick mind for assimilation and study, together with a strong urge to make good use of them.

To go on with the list, we come to that extraordinary personality of his, with its sense of complete independence of everybody. It serves him superbly: it is the keystone of the arch that is Beecham, the organizing genius of all the less divine array of gifts—that heavenly endowment which, for most of us, our careless angel forgot to distribute. Not personality only, but that precious gift of organizing the others and bringing them to full flower. Needless to say that his superb refusal to be worried by worldly cares seems always to be accepted as final. Argument, like his stick, may be dispensed with.

Even among the greatest musicians it may be that a vision that is clear in the mind does not find an outlet. Nothing of the sort with Beecham. Not only can he express what is in his mind, but the inward vision always seems to come to him at the right moment—when he has an orchestra before him. He is not one of those fated to be visited by inspiration only at inconvenient times, when use cannot be made of it.

All the way along this extraordinary man has apparently had things his own way. Not only is it given him to have this inward vision at his beck and call, but he seems to hold it as long as he will and weave his own fancies around it; it is no mere fleeting picture, lasting but a second and not to be recaptured.

Still not content with commandeering these heavenly treasures, he runs off with a composer for his own exclusive use. It is beside the point to label Beecham as the greatest exponent of Delius; the simple fact is that Delius's music was written for one man only to create. All his music-making is in a way creative for those in the orchestra, no matter what composer he is dealing with. He must—his instinct and nature leave him no other course—he must create.

Intellectual control of the emotion, which raises some artists to their greatest height in interpretative art, would kill Beecham. The essence of his power lies in the absolutely unfettered expression of his feelings, which seem to live at the very root of music. Because he is creative in his work, he is not strictly to be reckoned among the conductors who may be termed virtuosi. The greatest power of these

34

lies simply in producing superb orchestral playing, their consummate knowledge of the orchestra enabling them, with the help of the composer, to charm and thrill both orchestra and audience. Nor is he to be included among the pure idealists, who incessantly seek after the mind of their composer for the truest interpretation of his thoughts, and place both the orchestra and themselves in a secondary position.

Beecham is neither; he is like Kipling's cat that walked by himself. He is a music-maker who bows the knee to none, and whom all must serve who wish to work with him. If the whole mighty procession of the great composers were to pass before him, he would doff his bowler to them but the gesture would not be untouched by irony.

There is Beecham in every bar of his interpretations, but it is also pure music. The one is the counterpart of the other. Where some conductors stamp their personalities on the composer, and almost shout their mis-interpretations—"This is *my* Beethoven"—"Listen to *my* Brahms"—Beecham's performances electrify us by his own personification of music. One is not so much conscious of Mozart, Sibelius, Strauss, or whoever the composer may be, as that here is sheer, fascinating music, with a hint of magic. No matter who the composer, fascinating music will come forth, provided Beecham feels deeply enough about the work. It may not be a realization of the composer's intention; in a work of grand design, for instance, the architecture may be reduced in majesty of effect. But whatever the result the performance will be alive, extraordinarily vivid. No orchestra has ever found Beecham dull.

He appears ill at ease only when he by chance finds himself directing a work with which he is not in sympathy. If his feelings are not touched by a piece of music, then it is a waste of time for him to play it, for his music-making is then failed by the inspiration without which it is nothing —the notion of compromise is not in his character. In music as in life he does or does not, entirely in accordance with his own will. If certain music touches him he plays it, and all he needs from the composer is a general indication of tempo, balance and expression. But with scores that are marked in every detail by a composer who knows to a fraction his own mind—like Elgar's symphonies, for instance —Beecham has to curb his own creative sense and seems to find insufficient latitude for his feelings. It is significant that names such as Elgar, Holst and Mahler, composers who leave implicit instructions in their scores, seldom appear in his programmes. What if he were to tackle a score by one of the Schönbergians, who insist not only upon undeviating obedience by the conductor to microscopic details but also that conductor and orchestra shall digest a glossary of new technical terms! Beecham's opening words to the orchestra at the first rehearsal can be imagined:—

"Gentlemen of the Orchestra,

"I trust you have studied the composer's dictionary (which you will doubtless have observed on the front page of your parts) with the same amount of attention as I have lavished upon the score. I propose, therefore, that with your pencils, your—ah—most indelible pencils, you delete meticulously every mark of the composer's. We will allow him but the virgin notes on the stave, with which we shall do precisely what we like."

Having him now on the rostrum we may note that the slow and majestic tread with which he has approached it has made its contribution to the power he wields over his audience. This is exerted by his first step on the platform. His portentous approach to the rostrum and stately ascent are the same at every rehearsal, and if he is a guest-conductor he probably will at his first rehearsal express in a few words his pleasure at meeting the orchestra. If he has not seen the hall or studio for some time and observes any alteration, a droll remark may be expected.

His utterance is clear-cut and somewhat drawled, with an accent that is only Beecham's. Most characteristic when he is being supercilious or poking fun, it is indescribable though not by any means inimitable. His speech is always musical. Not so his singing voice. Of the queer varieties of the vocal art exemplified by conductors, Beecham's is surely the least expressive. It is the only vehicle of his expression which serves him badly. By gestures or words he can convey what he is driving at with no difficulty whatever; but if he tries to sing. . . .! He starts on no recognizable note and invariably ascends in pitch when he should drop, and *vice versa*. His entire compass seems to lie between four notes around middle C—an inadequate equipment for singing the opening phrase of 'Heldenleben'. And still, without any natural gift for singing, he conveys something with his efforts.

It used to be a debated question in the orchestras in his younger days whether he ever troubled to study a score beforehand, or whether he left it until the actual rehearsal, relying on assimilating it then with his incredible high-speed memory. He once remarked: "Gentlemen, I know very little about this work—I shall follow you." Next night at the concert he played from memory. Beecham's memory has become a legend. Here is a story typical of his readiness for anything. He turned up one night at the theatre—it was during one of his seasons before the War—and decided on the spur of the moment that he would conduct. Arriving at his place when the overture was due to begin, he leant over to his leader: "We are performing 'Figaro' to-night, are we not?" "Oh no, Sir Thomas," said the leader, "it is 'Seraglio'." "My dear fellow, you amaze me!" With that he closed the score on his desk and proceeded to perform the opera from memory.

Such stories date back to the early phases of his career when his attendance at rehearsals was somewhat erratic. Nowadays a very few minutes' grace is all he generally allows himself, but then an hour was not an uncommon allowance for him. One day in Manchester he had arranged for an extra, safety-first rehearsal immediately before a Hallé concert. The orchestra turned up at 5.30, waited and waited, at last grew restive, and then left the hall, putting a large notice on the conductor's desk—"Back at 7."

An eleventh-hour rehearsal which no one will forget who took part in it was before a performance of 'Solomon' at Queen's Hall with the copyists' ink not yet dry on the paper, the parts full of mistakes, and barely enough of them finished to make the concert possible. The hall, the artists' room, probably the organ loft too, were overrun with copyists and littered with manuscript, while the doorkeepers kept the audience out of the hall, until they were swept aside at 7.50 p.m.

Beecham dresses immaculately. His button boots are his only peculiarity. Indeed, although he is completely a law to himself in all things, musical and unmusical, he is so conventional as to wear stiff collars at rehearsals.

In a quarter of an hour they are rags, for he works in a way that wets him through. Some Continental conductors wear special clothes for their work, which may be anything from a white linen umpire's coat to a neat affair in alpaca.

Beecham's magic as a conductor lies in his consummate ability to express his inmost feelings through his personality. He is never seen to labour under any difficulty, and though his actions on the rostrum suggest to outsiders sometimes those of a ballet dancer rather than a conductor, yet those very actions are a perfect expression of himself. Not a gesture is studied; each extravagance is a perfectly natural outward sign of the music in his own heart. He would find it as impossible to be still and controlled on the rostrum, like Weingartner, or to disguise himself as an ordinary man. That extraordinary personality, exerting an almost hypnotic sway on orchestra and audience alike, has made him the great conductor. He obtains his results from sheer magnetism, and not from the accredited art of the conductor—stick-technique.

Beecham's stick describes all the antics of an erratic firework. One moment it is motionless, his only movement a crooking of one finger in his left hand; the next, his whole body is in furious action, with both fists threatening the orchestra. He breaks every orthodox rule. No one else in the world could get away with it as he does.

It is generally accepted by orchestras that a conductor's baton has a moment in its flight when it "clicks" for action. That may be anywhere, provided that the orchestra knows the arranged spot; after five minutes of rehearsal this is generally clear enough. Beecham refuses to be bound to any such rigid method. The orchestra has no notion where his stick is going; yet something about the whole man flashes and a perfect result is achieved, like a conjuring trick. He does unheard-of things at moments where the music touches a climax; thus, for great *tutti* chords he will flash up and give a direct indication for the attack a full quarter of a beat too soon. Yet the effect he produces is a perfect attack with an almost superhuman urgency about it.

Even though his magnetism is as prodigious as his memory, it must not be thought that he is easy to follow. Orchestras with whom he appears as a guest-conductor find it nearly impossible at times to discover that vital beat which ensures order out of chaos. Naturally he needs an orchestra that is really his, one that can grow up in his methods, or lack of them. Nevertheless, he can get anything he likes even from a strange orchestra. In a brilliant piece of Sibelius's like 'Lemminkainan', when both his arms are thrashing like flails, the orchestral players become like aeroplane pilots "flying blind"—hanging on for grim death. The effect to the audience, however, is apparently electric and clear, to say nothing of the daemonic power he puts into it. Notwithstanding his superb confidence, he said a few words of warning to the orchestra about this piece: "Gentlemen, in this piece you may find it a matter of some difficulty to keep your places. I think you might do well to imagine yourselves disporting in some hair-raising form of locomotion such as Brooklands, or a switchback railway. My advice to you is merely, Hold tight, and do not let yourselves fall off. I cannot guarantee to help you on again."

His baton is not a time-beater, but serves him as his chief instrument for describing the music itself. As often as not he will indicate the rhythm with his left hand. The opening and shutting of his outstretched hand is a typical indication of his for a "sharp beat", when he is particularly desirous of perfect ensemble, while his stick will describe the whole curve and every nuance of a phrase. All his actions are considerably more sharply defined and compelling at the concert, many of them at rehearsal having been almost vague. He listens most intently at his first rehearsals, and does not "direct" until the spade-work is done. A short account of some of his rehearsing in Delius's 'Paris' will show this kind of thing.

A Haydn symphony, 'Paris', Grieg's pianoforte concerto, and two pieces from Sibelius's suite 'Karelia' may be considered a typical Beecham programme. The Haydn and Delius take up three-quarters of the time he spends on rehearsal. Both works he has played time and time again, but he tackles them with fresh outlook. Where many conductors give the orchestra the impression of stereotyped performances of works continually in their programmes, Beecham sets out on a new journey each time, and is seldom heard to say: "I generally make an allargando here," or "In this passage I always like the flute to stand out." On the contrary, from the opening bar of his first rehearsal he seems to be weaving new patterns in his mind, especially in a work of phantasy like 'Paris'.

Gazing round the orchestra at his first rehearsal he finds the players placed in an unaccustomed way. "Gentlemen, you are doubtless—ah—used to the queer positions in which I find you, and in time I shall presumably locate one or two of you. I should like the bass clarinet to give some slight indication of his presence by holding up his hand—thank you! Now perhaps, with the help of the contra-fagotto, you will be kind enough to induct us into the lights and —ah—mysteries of 'Paris'."

He plays the entire work through, sitting on his usual raised chair, listening most intently, occasionally making curt comments:—

"Clarinet—'Cello, a little more, please—in six—Basses lighter—fliute," (he always pronounces flute thus—fliute). At the same time he strengthens these comments by a gesture of his stick towards the particular instrument. Stopping only once, for a slight misunderstanding at the *molto adagio*—"In six, please!"—and then once more at the end, when the little pan-pipe call on the piccolo (off-stage) goes awry, and leads him to remark, *sotto voce*, to the principal violin—"Who did that?" The piccolo complains that there is no one to keep the door open for him, and if it is shut he cannot see the beat. Whereupon Beecham—"My dear fellow, I will see that the entire staff of attendants of the Queen's Hall are put at your disposal to-morrow night, or if they cannot cope with the matter, I will personally break the door down!"

When he finishes the piece he touches on the various points that have arisen. "Gentlemen, that was very good on the whole; I have little to suggest in the beginning. But at No. 4, basses, a little more, please; something between *mezzo-piano* and *mezzo-forte*; a rather heavy sound is required there. At No. 5, oboe and clarinet, I should like you to play that vulgar tune a little harder—in fact, a demonstration of good vulgar spirits in the early morning, which our friends on the Continent seem to enjoy.

"Fifth bar before No. 7, violas and clarinets, a little more distinct, that phrase, if you please. Second violins, a little quieter when you start your quavers after Fig. 8—it was too loud for you to make a proper crescendo. At the *con moto* before Fig. 12 the gentlemen with the quavers are requested to play lightly. Now, at Fig. 13, I want the following instruments to stand out—7th and 8th bar, clarinet; 9th bar, oboe; 10th, clarinet again; and the accompanying instruments are to play quietly, if you please. Now let us play once more as far as Fig. 13."

This time he listens less intently, and begins to direct the playing with more decision, stopping to clear up more details, and taking freer *tempi*. At a stop for further detail he mentions Fig. 6. "Gentlemen, I do not intend to bother about the passage at No. 6. It has never been heard yet, and I doubt whether it ever will be." He goes on in the same manner to No. 13, then—"Violas, not too much *crescendo* in your first bar, and then *diminuendo* to help you to build up your phrase right up to the top. Reserve your transports for that note, if you please, and not before. And at the five semiquavers at the end of your phrase, I should like a shade more tone, and *molto diminuendo*, so that they fade into the next bar, and together, please." He plays on, and continually stops for corrections.

At the *molto adagio* he draws out the first violin phrase and moves on again in each alternate bar. The harp semi-quavers have to be fitted in from Beecham's back view, as best they can, for he turns full to the 1st violins for the whole of this passage. At a stop at Fig. 18 he speaks to the 'cello and 1st horn. "'Cello, in your solo you must listen to the horn, who shares your tune—in this case his sound will travel down to you quicker than yours to him, whatever the acoustical experts may say. Now I want this solo played very free, with a slight quickening of the tempo at the beginning of each bar, and making up for it at the ends. At Fig. 19, cymbals, a grand smash of your delightful instrument to help in the general welter of sound, if you please!"

In the next passage he asks for special care over the climax, which should be two bars before Fig. 20, and not at the *prestissimo*. He plays this several times—from the *tranquillo* to Fig. 22—working up both tempo and fire, until he is satisfied that the orchestra will respond to any of his demands, which may never be quite the same. This terrific feeling of stress he keeps up at white heat right into the march theme at Fig. 23. This march, at the first rehearsal, was comparatively subdued, both as to tempo and power (at the concert he swung it along with the theme *fff* and considerably quicker), and then he suddenly shuts off the sound, like a sharply shut window, for the solo violin passage in octaves with flute and bassoon. Momentum is again regained until the *ritenuto* before Fig. 25, and he ends the episode with a terrific crash on the two G flat chords, which he rehearses once or twice for sufficient attack and power.

Three bars after the ensuing *meno mosso* he stops again.

"Gentlemen in the clarinet department, how can you resist such an impassioned appeal from the second violins? Give them an answer, I beg you!"

This three-bar sentence, starting in the second violins, followed by clarinets and concluded by solo violin and 1st horn, is the kind of thing Beecham creates out of Delius —three entirely separate ideas, woven into an intensely expressive sentence that is full of the tenderest feeling, yet is never allowed to become sentimental or sickly.

At the *adagio molto* after Fig. 27 he beats eight, giving the oboe the utmost freedom to enjoy a *tenuto* on his top A and B flat, before his descending semiquavers, the whole of the accompaniment being hushed to a whisper. Having rehearsed a clear change of harmony on the last chord before Fig. 28, he bustles on to a similar climax at Fig. 30, making the top three bars before Fig. 31, and demanding still more force at the bar after Fig. 32. The tempo at Fig. 33 is still kept up to the *allegretto grazioso*, and only subsides gradually. No. 34 he takes in six, in *tempo rubato*, with a good deal of space between the quavers at the end of the bar, but the bassoons and horns have to move in strict tempo in the next bar. The same thing happens, only more quietly, in the strings' next phrase, the following two bars subsiding into the quietest sound from the bassoon and bass clarinet. After a break, the string chords fade, each one less, into nothing. He makes a point for the flute at this spot. "That

tune of yours, flute, I want it played as if you heard someone whistling, walking away from you in the street, and
suddenly turning a corner, when he gets to your second D.
I hope the piccolo has now succeeded in opening his door!"
(He sounds cheerful enough.)

"Well, gentlemen, I will now play the Haydn, so the rest
of you may enjoy your siesta—or whatever else you can
enjoy in this benighted country!"

These rehearsals of Beecham's gather intensity, and there
is nearly always a difficulty in finishing to time, for the more
he gets inside a work the more there is to be done, especially
when he finishes a last rehearsal with a Haydn or Mozart
symphony. He leaves the actual polish until the last
moment. When it comes to the concert, although he is
intensely wrapped up in the music, he is very much alive
to every extraneous happening, whether it is a banged seat,
a late-comer or an error in the orchestra. But nothing on
this earth would put him off. There was a slight discrepancy
in the very introduction of this Haydn symphony, which
opened the concert, and although he instantly sensed it,
nothing showed in his expression.

His face is amazingly compelling, and the intensity of his
expression is eloquent enough to reflect his feelings without
much else. Beecham at a concert becomes a sheer personification of the music he is performing. Every part of him
seems associated with its vitals, and every gesture or facial
expression the result of feelings that know no rein.

SIR ADRIAN BOULT

SIR ADRIAN BOULT

AMONG the contemporary conductors of international fame, Adrian Boult represents Idealism. He is an idealist in his incessant striving after the most faithful approximation possible to the composer's mind. It is an essentially different attitude from that of the conductor whose principal aim is the finest possible playing and who, almost necessarily therefore, uses a composition as a vehicle for his own art rather than as a source of inspiration.

Adrian Boult's quiet stance on the rostrum, the economy of his gesture and his general stillness give a strong impression of restraint. His rigid self-control is no studied pose but the man himself. Disliking all forms of showmanship, he prefers to be an almost impersonal medium between the composer, orchestra and audience rather than the central character of a drama. His mind seems to brood over the score from a height, surveying all its essential features like the peaks of a mountain range seen from a certain distance. The proportions are thus truly discerned, with the greatest peaks duly towering above the rest. This amounts to saying that Boult is at his best in musical compositions that can be said to have architectural character, and is less at ease in the slighter music of phantasy and colour.

This "idealistic" attitude quite frequently entails a departure from traditions—the traditions that have only too often been formed in the course of years by a succession of conductors who held personal success to be more important than loyalty to the scores in hand. There are musical compositions which, in whole or part, are regularly played in a way that—however regardless of the composer's intention—can be counted upon to tickle the public fancy, until in the long run a false tradition is firmly established.

But at rehearsals Boult will characteristically say: "No *crescendo*! If the composer had wanted one there he would have put one in." Or, again, when rehearsing some much-edited work of Bach: "Take out all those slurs! It is only one of those infernal editors again—there is no trace of anything of the sort in the original."

The 'Figaro' overture is more often than not played at breakneck pace, and brings the house down by the virtuosity of the playing. But with Boult it is the crotchets that are *presto*, not the minims, though he, of course, beats two in a bar. As this is Mozart's own indication he prefers it to a more brilliant display.

On the subject of balance Boult is inexhaustible. He obtains his results by a very close study of the score and by persuading the players to use their intelligence to read between the lines of their parts with an alert ear for other instruments. If they are sitting too far from one another to hear adequately, then they must learn to know what is happening and adjust their tone accordingly. Balanced playing he regards as not solely the conductor's concern, but also one in which the players must take an active and intelligent interest. Faulty balance is at times the cause of an explosion. Thus:

"How on earth can you expect the clarinet to play his

tune decently when you are lumbering along underneath like that? For goodness' sake, listen! Keep alive!" Mild enough words, no doubt; but there is plenty of meaning in the voice.

He attaches particular importance to the balance as judged by the broadcast effect, and looks upon the microphone as a valuable gauge. In his view, the balance, if right for the microphone, will certainly be right in the hall. On the other hand, what will do in the hall is not necessarily good enough for the microphone. He consequently makes full use of the B.B.C.'s Balance and Control Department, requiring of it confirmation of doubtful points in rehearsals for public concerts as well as studio performances.

Another characteristic of his rehearsals is his insistence upon rhythmic swing. Scarcely a rehearsal is without resort to this expression. Rhythmic swing he regards as the very life of musical performance, and nothing so much exasperates him as a wooden accent mechanically bumping on the first of the bar.

"No, no! It all sounds dead. Do swing the rhythm over from the end of each second bar to the third, and so on! Only be careful when the bar-groups alter in the 10th bar." This kind of thing also happens on the last note of a phrase, as in the opening of Mozart's G minor symphony where the first violins go over to their B flat.

"Firsts, be careful! That B flat sounds the loudest note in the phrase. I want to hear it; but don't sit down on it so hard!" But although for ever insisting upon vital rhythm he does not fail to warn the players against self-conscious rhythm—the rhythm that is applied without being felt. All, in truth, that he wants is the style in which every chamber player is brought up.

Another aspect of style—the cultivation of the characteristic style proper to different composers or schools—forms an important study in his training of the orchestra. The differences are naturally subtle, but to the great breadth of a Brahms phrase he gives a certain character that is the very antithesis to what he requires in a similar phrase in Franck's symphony. He conceives the French schools as demanding an almost exaggerated attention to neatness and compactness of phrasing, with rhythmic figures generally as crisp as possible, while in Schumann and Brahms everything is required to be broad and spacious, while at the same time held well in control. But restraint is largely relinquished in Russian music, and here he stimulates violent changes of mood and colour.

The re-scoring of doubtful passages, especially in the classics, he utterly eschews, and nonetheless, by great care in the subsidiary parts, he nearly always succeeds in establishing the essential line. If a wood-wind player has to complain that he has already been blowing "fit to burst" there is trouble for somebody. When, in the last resort, something really has to be done—in Beethoven, for instance —Weingartner's authority is sought. But this happens very rarely.

In Brahms practically no dynamic mark is allowed to be altered. Only, if the orchestra is large enough, the wood-wind is skilfully doubled. Results of remarkable clarity are obtained by complete but wary adherence to the score. The dynamic marks of all composers prior to Rimsky-

Korsakov and Elgar have naturally to be treated with a caution from which the more scrupulous moderns relieve the conductor. Brahms, for instance, impartially marks *forte* or *piano*, as the case may be, for all instruments, regardless of their difference of power. Boult, then, directs that the trumpet shall modify its *forte*, when it is necessary to match the horn; and so on, throughout the orchestra. Elgar, on the other hand, made allowances for this in his scrupulous markings, and Boult plays Elgar's scores quite literally.

Springing from the roots of his nature is Boult's humane consideration for the orchestra. It would be profoundly wrong to regard this as the sign of an easy-going character. It is really sound psychology, as well as the result of an appreciation of other people's feelings. He knows his players and can safely count upon them to give as intelligently as they can. Thus he avoids the orchestra's most dreaded bugbear—that vain repetition at rehearsals which breeds boredom, exasperation and ultimately inefficiency and staleness.

Boult's general rehearsal method is—in a symphony, for instance—to play, if possible, as far as the end of the exposition without stopping. Having an excellent memory, he can bear in mind the salient points calling for criticism; with the orchestra at rest he then discusses these points for a few moments. The passages criticized are now severally played but not, as a rule, the whole. Boult's rehearsals are a means to an end. Each one becomes a little more tense, but never does he aim at a peak until the performance proper. He holds physical freshness to be of more moment than any great achievement at rehearsal. He may require certain passages to be played with full power for the purpose of balance, but that power must be still greater "on the night."

"Horns, I don't want you to spoil your lip now, but everything you've got, to-night!" And again: "You see that the trombones don't support you at that point. You must carry the weight of the whole orchestra yourselves". —a characteristic sentence, in that it gives the players a clear reason for the demand made. Boult invites the orchestra to use its understanding in the performance of music. He does not look upon his players as mere cogs in a machine.

Boult is exceptionally still on the rostrum. He seems quite comfortable with about six inches of room on either side of him, and he never moves his feet. Every movement he makes is controlled; he relies almost entirely on the stick itself, which often follows the line of the phrase in a curve and rises just a fraction before the bar-line to make clear the swing. His left hand is used sparingly and never unnecessarily.

In pianissimo his stick scarcely moves at all, and it has then to be very carefully watched by those who are some distance away. For the really great moments his right hand will go back behind his body with an extra effort, but only at the top of a climax. That is his strength. By restraint and complete control over his own emotions and temperament and those of the orchestra he doubles his power when it is all wanted. And let no one think that he is too fond of the leash. Listen, for instance, to the 'Flying Dutchman' overture under his direction. At those moments marked by Wagner for special fury, the winds scream with far more violence than is felt if the utmost is made of the top of every chromatic scale.

'Leonora No. 3' comes naturally to mind as an illustration of Boult's methods at rehearsal, for nothing better shows his attitude as a faithful interpreter. It is the antithesis to the performances by conductors who so stamp their own personalities on the score that the effect is less Beethoven than a fantasy on a Beethoven theme. Boult seeks to impress Beethoven's mind upon the orchestra, and succeeds as few conductors do.

At rehearsal the first unison G has to be accurately balanced and corrected for faults of intonation in the wind, and the long *diminuendo* that follows over four bars has to be played until it really becomes a steady dwindling of tone. The *crescendo* in the next bar of the strings may go too far, or else the *diminuendo* begins too soon. "Up to the end of the third quaver strings only, or we shall never hear the bassoons!"

The semiquaver triplet passage between the flute and first violins goes a little awry. "Firsts, be careful that there is no gap after Mr. X's F sharp! It's always a bit late, and I want it to fit perfectly, as one arpeggio between you.—No! It's not together yet, firsts, but it is the early people who are right!"

In the bar before the big A flat major chord the trombones perhaps enter too loudly and so spoil the gradual *crescendo* already begun by the wood-wind. "Trombones, be careful to balance your tone with the wood-wind.

Remember, they've only got up to *mf* on your entry. I want the tone built up steadily to the *fff*s."

After two or three shots at the A flat string passages for more brilliance, and then a good attack on the following chords, the little demi-semiquavers at the end of the bar are perhaps out of place. "Strings, they must be absolutely in place on the last semiquaver of the bar. Count four on that last beat!"

At the end of the *adagio* he probably finds it necessary to play it through all again, but then does not stop until the trumpet fanfare. Here, when he brings the orchestra to a standstill, he does not succeed in stopping the trumpet, who is, of course, off stage. "All right, Mr. X! Oh, tell him, somebody. We must stop here—there is rather a lot that wants seeing to. First of all, it isn't alive, and you are not all listening. Several wood-wind tunes were lost. Wind, those chords on the off-beats were all over the place. They must be on time, to fit the violin octaves.

"Strings, at the opening of the *allegro* you simply sat on those dotted minims, and then bumped your last crochet of each phrase. Think of the tune in two-bar groups, with perhaps the slightest push at the beginning of each alternate bar. Basses, be careful too of your C's. Don't make them all alike!

"Then the great *crescendo* never really grew at all. You had used everything up before you got to the *ff*, which, incidentally, was a very poor affair. And I want still more power five bars later. Don't *crescendo* immediately you see it marked—remember how far you have to go, and make an absolutely steady piling-up to the crash at the *ff*. And at the *sempre ff*, five bars later, all you're worth!

"Violins and seconds, not too much *crescendo* on those accompanying triplet figures! They were altogether too heavy. And, all of you, please let me do as I like at the *pianissimo* bars later on. Some of you crashed in too soon at those repeated quavers. Those three silent beats are mine, and you will kindly not encroach on my private property. Strings, there was no attack at all on the scales leading up to the trumpet. I want a terrific attack after that quaver rest, and I make no pull up whatever."

After one or two things have been put straight he starts again just before the fanfare, but bad articulation of the little rhythmic figure in the strings makes him stop and speak to the leader.

"Mr. X, I want those rhythmic figures clearer and yet dead *pp*. Can you get it better for me?"

Mr. X's reply is to the effect that some of the players are not ready with their bows on the string, and also it is better to use the point of the bow. All then goes well, perhaps, until the run-up of the flute at the return, when the strings are admonished for being too loud. The violin cadenza makes him mutter, "We'll see to that later." The *crescendo* at the end, again, is unsatisfactory, and he directs that the tone is not to be dropped at the place usually marked *mf*, since the trombones enter there and it is unnecessary. On the other hand, a slight drop to help the *crescendo* may be made four bars later, when the trombones stop. The *crescendo* is then piled up to *fff* (the one *f* can be ignored). This climax crowns the whole work, and must be made

57   E

even more intense than the A flat chord in the introduction and the first *ff* in the *allegro*. "Last of all, don't play all the chords at the end alike. Make the last one the biggest!"

In tackling new works Boult will do his utmost to get the composers to be present, at least for one rehearsal, in spite of the fact that they frequently upset the timing and are apt to be difficult. But provided they know their own minds, all goes well. If he cannot, as in the case of 'Wozzeck', have the composer, he obtains, for fear of misreading the composer's directions, the presence of some authority like Herr Prerauer of Berlin, who first produced 'Wozzeck'.

It has often been noticed that Boult not only knows the complicated scores of Schönberg, Bartók, Berg and the like from beginning to end, but can also make them intelligible to his orchestra without any agitation or extra rehearsal. When foreign specialists come over to conduct them their knowledge is apparently no deeper; they have infinite difficulty in making themselves understood, even with a good interpreter, and invariably have to be helped out with longer or extra rehearsals. To say nothing of an exasperated orchestra into the bargain.

It is a feature of Boult's technique as a conductor, this quick assimilation of scores in every kind of idiom. He finds his way about quickly, and is able to take the orchestra with him straight to the root of the matter. He organizes both other people and himself, smoothly and without fuss or agitation; and although his repertory covers the whole realm of orchestral music, he conducts most of the well-known works from memory. It is significant that when

Toscanini conducted the B.B.C. Orchestra in 1935, in his rehearsals he scarcely touched Brahms's fourth symphony or the 'Enigma' variations—two of Boult's greatest interpretations. He was indeed able actually to cut down the allowance of rehearsal time—a tribute to Boult's orchestra training.

Being an Englishman, without any natural showmanship or the prima donna's temperament usually found in famous conductors, Boult may possibly never become a popular idol, but there are few conductors in the world who surpass him in the art of true interpretation.

PAU CASALS

PAU CASALS

FOR all musicians Casals is the supreme 'cellist and master of interpretation. Playing under his baton one cannot help feeling a little sad that he is not using his own instrument. Interesting he must always be, whenever he makes music; yet he does not hold the orchestra in the same way as when he is actually playing a phrase with that inimitable style that places him above all other 'cellists and is unsurpassed by any string player.

If Casals cannot explain to his orchestra exactly what is in his mind, and as his stick never approaches the art of his superb bow for the delineation of a phrase, it is scarcely to be expected that any human being gifted with perfect expression in a particular medium should succeed equally with one that is widely different. An instrumentalist is at only one remove from a singer for sheer, direct expression, but the conductor's art is indirect and depends upon the play of his own mind over many others. Such a difficulty as language may seriously interfere with the smooth passing of his ideas to his players. Casals himself has a good command of English, but often he fails to get the response he wishes because he cannot easily express it in words or by his stick. He is forced to spend much of his time singing, and this, except for the expression of an actual phrase, is inadequate and frequently ambiguous.

He has powerful and penetrating eyes, which are made

all the more compelling through magnifying glasses, but they do not seem to have that property of transmitting his mind which Toscanini's and Beecham's can flash to their players. His own orchestra at Barcelona has been the grand passion of his life, and he has made the 'cello both his servant and theirs. At times he seems almost to hate having to play it—it is an effort, and on his appearance as conductor after playing a concerto he says: "Ah, what a relief! I can enjoy making music with you now!"

With his own orchestra he works very much for the love of the thing, and the time-factor comes very little into the matter at all. Hence he is always rather worried in London at being allowed only three rehearsals. "Ah, ladies and gentlemen, some conductors are modest, yes! They want only one hour to rehearse a piece. Me, I like a year, and then I am not finished! I am never finished; always there is something more to say."

At Barcelona they used to go on rehearsing to all hours of the night for the fun of the thing, Casals subsidizing the whole undertaking himself. Now, since the catastrophe of 1936, he has lost almost everything, and has decided that everything he still possesses or can do shall be placed at the service of his country. One of the most moving things ever said to any orchestra was his short speech after being welcomed to the B.B.C. in 1937. When he appeared for the first rehearsal of Elgar's 'cello concerto it was obvious he had passed through a period of terrible strain. In a halting voice, not only hesitant with the effort of speaking English again, he said: "I am glad, more than glad, to be amongst you again. You know what outrageous things have been happening in my own country. To be in a civilized country again means so much. You in England have so far escaped these terrible dangers, and you must know this: All the hopes of other countries lie in England! I must go back in one or two days; my country needs me and I must be there. For the moment I look forward to making music with you, and I hope you will enjoy it too!"

Whenever he is the solo 'cellist, the strings of the orchestra listen as to no one else. The atmosphere is something like that of a Toscanini rehearsal. Only a supreme master can command that extra interest, and no other 'cellist can hold an accompanying orchestra as Casals does. Not only is his tone completely individual, but the divine simplicity of his phrasing and musicianship shows his greatness in every note he plays. Technique never protrudes; the 'cello sounds in his hands a natural and delightfully easy instrument. The acute difficulties of intonation and all the other technical problems seem not to exist for him. Whatever feats of dexterity he may be performing, the music is always foremost and is never obscured by them.

This vision for true interpretation is his passion in music-making, and it will easily be understood that the 'cello's repertory limits him too narrowly. With so much great music written for the orchestra, why should he, because he is a 'cellist, be denied the interpretation of it? It must be galling for the superb artist that he is to be limited always to the same old works—Haydn, Schumann, Dvořák, Strauss's 'Don Quixote' and so on. Yet because of his unique art, these are the works that the world desires of him. (Apparently, with the exception of Tovey's concerto, the more modern works do not appeal to him as filling the gaps that the great masters have left.) But conducting opens up to him the whole realm of great music.

At heart he is also a great teacher and he loves imparting his knowledge of interpretation to the orchestra. He will spend hours on a movement of a symphony, dwelling on phrase after phrase for subtle detail. Unfortunately the orchestra often finds it impossible to grasp what he is striving for, and at times wish to heaven he would play it on the 'cello. His stick would be reckoned quite efficient in an ordinary conductor, but it is inadequate to express that magnificent mind of his. Frequently it lets him down, being somewhat indefinite. When ensemble goes a little awry he flaps both arms violently, but without sufficient grip to draw together the ragged ends. The stick may often be but is not always quite clear, and because of this the orchestra is never perfectly confident, particularly at the beginnings of movements and at changes of tempi. Part of the trouble is that his stick does not appear to come to rest at any point, and as often as not he will suddenly and disconcertingly take charge with his left hand.

When concentrating on a perfect attack he succeeds as well as any one; but, wrapped up in the music as he becomes, he is apt to forget that the orchestra is waiting for a vital gesture. All his interest is concentrated on the inwardness of the music, and hence the orchestral problems of balance and technique are of secondary importance to him. On the 'cello he has only to feel, and to be able to express himself thus is natural for him. But it is not so easy for him to express his thought through other minds. The orchestra needs something more than that he himself should be living in the music. With a great deal of rehearsal, and in his own language, the result probably is vastly different. Under our conditions it is felt that he is not able to achieve the half of what he would wish. He attempts to get round the difficulty of expressing exactly what is in his mind by repeatedly singing a phrase until the orchestra approaches his idea. Though exceptionally good and true, his voice cannot be expected to express a colour or a gradation as if he were playing.

"We mus' play—Ly-a-da-Ly-a-da-Ly-a-da—not Ly-a-da-Ly-a-da-Ly-a-da—no, it mus' be Ly-a-da-Ly-a-da-Ly-a-da." He will spend any amount of time demonstrating like this, sometimes with the orchestra little the wiser at the end of it all.

He invariably conducts in a woollen cardigan, and he brings with him a large bath-towel to cope with his perspiration. At the interval he winds a long woollen muffler round his neck and starts his pipe going. Even now he quickly becomes jaunty and cheerful when engaged in conducting, and enjoys every moment of his rehearsal. Delightful and charming in conversation, he is always ready for a word with members of the orchestra.

When playing the 'cello Casals nearly always seems to have his eyes closed, but while he conducts they are very wide open, and any thing or sound that displeases him causes them to turn straight in the direction of the miscreant, and, magnified by his powerful glasses, the look goes straight through one. Casals's smile is charming, and vanishes more quickly than it appears. One moment he will be enjoying a little joke, and then in a flash his face will become dead serious, as if a smile could never possibly grow there. If the music is light and happy his air will be jaunty and carefree, but if the mood is dark, as at the opening of Brahms's C minor symphony, he will look darker and more portentous than the glowering sky of the movement itself.

There is no aloofness about him, and relations with his own orchestra at Barcelona must be extremely happy and intimate. There is no feeling of strain in the air as there is when he is the 'cellist. Because the actual technicalities of the orchestra seem not to matter to him very much he brings no carefully marked parts with him. It might be expected that his string parts would be fully edited with his own ideas of bowing and phrasing, but actually they are far from comprehensive and much is left to the inspiration of the moment. Nothing delights the strings of the orchestra more than to study an edition by a master's hand, but Casals's parts are haphazard affairs and not even unanimous—nothing like the meticulously marked copies of Mengelberg or Koussevitsky. Actually it is surprising how little particular care he spends on any of the string departments when all the players would be only too glad of his lessons. One may have looked forward to his handling of a great 'cello tune in a Brahms symphony, as a pupil to an intimate lesson from the greatest of masters, but Casals does little more than any other fine conductor in moulding a phrase. No priceless secrets of tone-production, bow-control or left hand come forth. He is far too interested in the music of the phrase to bother about the technical process of its production, and he denies us a clue to the intensely personal secret of his own playing, except by showing us the mind that is behind it. With this he is generous, and his inimitable sense of *rubato* is shown clearly to everyone. His *rubato* is one of the chief joys he bestows on the orchestra. Because of his difficulties in making himself clear to them, the players are seldom able to give him unqualified satisfaction in this particular art, but nevertheless it is wonderful to see what he does with complete freedom, in a single bar or two of music, with the fundamental rhythm unaltered.

Of the features he particularly insists upon, the first notes of a phrase perhaps count first. He is always stopping for this. "No, we don' hear the first notes of the phrase. It mus' be there, it mus' sound always clear! Take care of the first note!"

When rehearsing 'Don Juan' he concentrated on this in every department. He tried very few passages by themselves until after the Love Scene, when he took 'celli and violas by themselves. Here everyone expected technical advice, but no. He just asked for the "first note" to be very clear, and for a correctly held minim, not to be hurried into the next bar, and the last crotchet to have no accent, but played very short. Apart from directing that the passage was to be played at the point of the bow in the usual manner, no other peculiarly technical help was given. He had these passages played repeatedly until they became clear and clean in intonation. His sense of pitch and intonation is intensely acute, and he allows no offence to pass. He does not pick out a bad note in a chord, but has it played until everyone listens more intently and it rights itself.

Saving time is not a practice of his; he is so used to æons of it at home that our three rehearsals—nine hours—for a concert of an hour and a quarter go nowhere with him. Making music with an orchestra is his joy. It matters little to him that the rehearsals are for the purpose of the concert; the music that is made at the rehearsal is just as important. From the idealistic point of view the rehearsals are meant for making better and better music, not just for a particular concert. That, for him, is only another rehearsal, as it were. He is absolutely sincere when he says he would like a year to rehearse for a concert—and that then it would not be perfect!

Perfection as a 'cellist he reached years ago, in our eyes, but not in his own, by a long way. All the farther, then, is he from his ideal when dealing with that more complex instrument, the orchestra. It is not only that the playing of an orchestra must always fall short of perfection, but there is also the score itself, which, if the work is a great one, has unfathomable depths for him. He is never, and never will be, finished with studying, and everything he studies he wishes to impart to his students in the orchestra. He looks upon the orchestra as his students; he is like a great surgeon demonstrating at a major operation.

Casals has no particular scheme for rehearsing, and does not portion out his time with any care. He picks up a score and remarks "Now we will take the Bach" (Brandenburg in F major). The parts seem to be in a muddle, and before beginning the leader asks him if the orchestra is to observe the somewhat vague bowing marks. "I am sorry, gentlemen, I have not all my own music with me, but we will do what we can—just make beautiful music together. It is not necessary to write all the bowing down; we must just understand, that is all! Very well, then"—and off he goes. He is always delighted with the result, after the concert, and has obviously enjoyed it thoroughly. "Oh, ye-es, it was excellent, but there are still many things, for me as well as you!"

The introduction having been played through, the leader asks him whether he wishes any further marks of expression put in the parts. "Oh, not *forte* the whole time, perhaps, but just an easy *mezzo forte*; as the phrases rise, so we will make a little natural *crescendo*, and then *diminuendo*, yes? But we mus' play with our own—intuition—is that the right word?—and it will be all right, yes!

"*Allegro*; now we mus' play this with an easy, frank rhythm. No hurrying, no pulling back! And the solo violin and the horn mus' look at me, yes? Because you are rather far apart, and I don' know about this studio—the acoustics? You probably both know the best place to sit, yourselves? Is there one behind the microphone who can tell me this?" The leader calls for Mr. S. "Ah," says Casals, "you know him, good!" (Much laughter.)

Minuet.—"No, you make bad bow-accent, on the third beat of the bar. It mus' not be this. Let me hear it again— no, it is still too heavy and monotonous. You mus' take care of the up bow and make it lighter, yes? Ah, that is better now."

Polacca.—A misunderstanding arose at the beginning of this movement. The beat seemed vague and indeterminate, nor could any direction be obtained from him as to the performance of the string quavers. At least three styles of bowing appeared in the different departments, and no ruling was eventually obtained.

The whole of this concerto suffered because of the parts, and it was surprising that, in a piece in which complete unanimity of the strings' style of bowing is all-important he should have almost ignored the matter. His attention is always on the 'music itself', and the line of the phrases and rhythm.

He spent most of his time on Schumann's symphony No. 3 in B flat. He again used unedited parts without bowings. The big opening phrase in the first violins, coupled with flutes, took him about twenty minutes to explain what he wanted, singing it over and over again, with a strong accent on the first dotted crotchet. The whole phrase was to be as *legato* as possible, and the accompanying repeated quavers to be played with as much care as the tune itself, supporting this accent and the whole line of the phrase.

The rehearsing of this opening was typical of Casals. No bowings were indicated at all, and where he could have obtained instant response by his own careful editing, he preferred to continue singing and singing—while the orchestra was far from unanimous in its interpretation of the subtleties of his vocal inflections.

His particular care over the first notes of phrases came again at the return of the quaver figure a few bars farther on. "I don' hear that first note, and the ensemble is not clear. Now let us play again from the *fortissimo*." This passage was played several times, also the semiquaver passages after the two dotted minims, eleven or twelve bars later. Two bars before A—the next *fortissimo*—he puts in a *piano* to help the *crescendo*. Six bars before B the semi-quavers are again not clear. "Ah, the first note again of your semiquavers; it is not *there*. Put an accent on it, in the first violins and violas!"

In the 5th and 6th bars, and 7th and 8th after the double bar, he asked for a long *diminuendo* in the 'celli and violas. The "natural" *diminuendo* is one of the few secrets allied with his actual 'cello playing that he gives away—that inimitable little *diminuendo* to the last note of a phrase. Nothing disturbs him more than an unmusical little bump there. He always ensures that the tone just lightens on it, as the note changes.

At the bar marked "*cresc.*" after letter L he directs "*piano*", and then builds up gradually to the *fff* over the whole twenty-two bars. In this movement, apart from the initial phrase, and these particular points of ensemble, he studies the general rhythmic impulse and building-up of the whole thing, rather than balance and detail of various sections. In the *scherzo* he once more seizes on the first note and sings the opening phrase repeatedly in a happy, exuberant spirit. "You mus' *not* accent the second note, no, it is the first one that mus' be heard."

Three or fours bars after letter D in the Trio show him again teaching that wonderful *diminuendo* of his to the seconds and violas. It is a very gradual *diminuendo* from the first note of the phrase to the very end of the last. Movement III: the beginning is played with a long *diminuendo* in the 4th and 5th bars—real Casals again. The whole movement is very free and almost conversational, *molto espressivo*. In the great viola tune before letter B he concentrates on playing *molto espressivo*. "If we play with enough expression these *rallentandi* are not necessary; in all music it is the same. We mus' try and avoid unnecessary *rallentandi*. And remember, falling phrase in *diminuendo*, yes?"

The last movement he did not rehearse much, but merely played it through once or twice. He is not very consistent, and it is often noticed that particular points stressed at the rehearsal are not necessarily observed at the concert. The *tempi*, of course, will nearly always be the same, and invariably seem to be obviously the correct ones. It is a wonderful experience, making music with him, and that is exactly what he strives for—not a brilliant performance, but just "to make beautiful music."

ALBERT COATES

ALBERT COATES

BORN at St. Petersburg in 1882, the son of a York-shireman who had settled in business there and married a Russian lady, Albert Coates is a cosmopolitan figure, with stronger Russian characteristics than English. He was sent to England for his education, eventually passing into Liverpool University as a science student, and at the same time studying music with an elder brother who held an organist's appointment at Liverpool. On returning to Russia he entered his father's office, but music had already called him too strongly and arrangements were made for him to go to the Leipzig Conservatory where he studied the 'cello under Klengel and the piano with Teichmüller. It was Nikisch, however, who fascinated him; and in his conducting class, Coates quickly found his trade. The 'cello and piano were soon abandoned to make way for his vocation as a conductor, which was sealed by his appointment to the Russian Imperial Opera at St. Petersburg, a post which he held until the Revolution.

He first became prominent in England in 1913, when he shared the Wagner performances at Covent Garden with Nikisch. But not until 1919 did he become really well-known to English musicians and audiences, at a series of concerts with the London Symphony Orchestra. He was then more Russian than English, and Russia must still take more than half the credit for his arresting personality and temperament. No conductor in the world is more impressive, and when he first appeared before English orchestras the players felt suddenly confronted with a Colossus. A man of immense proportions and commanding person; with the drive and power of a superman. All his ideas and actions are on a correspondingly large scale, and his intense, warmblooded temperament gives an unmistakable character to his performances. Terrific vitality, bulging *crescendi*, violent contrasts of colouring and great breadth of phrase are always features of his interpretations. His personality is too strong for him to sink himself entirely in the composer; but his bigness of conception generally outweighs the mere seeking of effects.

Russian music in particular takes on a vivid and arresting character in his hands, with restraint completely cast off and pent-up feelings allowed to run riot. Whether he is conducting an opera like Rimsky-Korsakov's 'Kitezh', a Tchaikovsky symphony, or a new work by, say Shostakovitch, the performance will have an intense feeling and grip that only a Russian can effect. Grip is Coates's first characteristic. He never loses it for an instant, though he is flexible enough not to hamper individual artistry. Players generally find themselves allowed considerable freedom— but if they go too far those beetling brows will gather and a furious look pulls them up short. He used rather to terrify some of the younger players, who were relieved not to be placed too near him. His face can become Tartar-like, and little imagination was needed to see oneself running for life from a violent Cossack giant. But that was only a fancy, principally made by his great size and by his animated facial expression that always reflects his feelings. Coates's predominant mood is jovial, and the enjoyment of life his keynote.

Work at rehearsals is strenuous but not over-exacting. Though Coates may not always ask for the last ounce, he spends all his own vitality. Within ten minutes of the beginning of a rehearsal, if the piece is at all vigorous, he will be throwing off cascades of perspiration. He gets hotter than any other conductor, and after a day's rehearsal the studio may resemble the drying-room of a laundry. He is never detached and aloof, either from the scores or the orchestra. Always he lives intensely in the midst of everything. It pleases him to be on fairly intimate terms with the orchestra and he usually calls some of the players by their Christian names; or failing that he will invent nicknames—an almost unheard-of thing in a famous guest-conductor.

"Come along, Blackie, what are you doing? I can't hear you, boy. Play it out!" The name was invented on the spur of the moment since he did not know the proper one, and the player had jet-black hair. He used at one time to take an almost childish pleasure in picking up a new name, and when the daughter of a well-known string leader married a distinguished violinist, Coates the next morning exclaimed: "Now then, father-in-law, your children are running all over the place. What's the matter? Do it again by yourselves from Letter B with the up beat. —Ah that's better!"

He has many characteristic gestures but never makes a fuss about them; they are all clear and purposeful. One that shows him to particular advantage is the slight tilting back of the head, while his mouth is opened wide to emphasize a deep breath for the brass, before an attack or sustained chord. He uses another very characteristic lead for a quick rhythmical passage needing strong impulse and grip to hold it together. Holding his arm high in front of his chest, he flicks his baton with an electric twist of his wrist, and if there is a long *crescendo* he gradually brings his whole arm to bear in a short throwing motion, emphasizing this with a similar movement of his left hand. It has the effect of a terrific impulse that is clearly seen by the whole orchestra. His habit is to hold his arms fairly high—a great advantage for those on the outskirts of the strings.

His face, strongly animated both in concert and rehearsal, insists upon warmth of feeling in response. Queen's Hall unheated on a Sunday morning was always a trial to him. Not so much that he feels the actual cold himself, but he loathes a cold sound from the orchestra and in particular from the strings.

"Good morning to you ull!" (a certain little foreign accent still shows in his English). "It's jolly to see old friends again and a perfect miracle every time we come together. I've been round the earth since I saw you last. Let's play the Delius pieces." After a few minutes' cold and flat playing, he breaks off to exclaim: "Oh that's no good! You're making a ghastly sound like a lot of ghosts. I suppose it's because your wretched hall is so cold. Throw away the Delius and let's hammer away at the 'Ride' to get warm. Blow on your fingers, do anything you like, but let's have some of that marvellous tone of yours!"

He is fond of getting the utmost out of the heavier

instruments, and from the percussion too. He shouts to this department at the top of a climax:

"Smash it, boy! Hit everything you can see. Don't be afraid of it! Brass, I want a burst of sound." And he opens his arms to the fullest extent of his reach and his mouth as for an enormous breath—a truly formidable sight!

He is quick to seize on any unevenness in a department, and in a brass passage such as at the end of the Pathetic Symphony he would warn that brilliant trombone player, the late Jesse Stamp: "Careful, Jesse, you're standing out of the picture too much! It sounds marvellous but keep it in, boy! No. 2 and 3, play up to him!"

Scriabin is a composer whose name will always be associated with Coates. He made Londoners familiar with several of Scriabin's works, of which he has an intimate knowledge. 'The Poem of Ecstasy' made him coin a phrase which he still uses frequently when he wants a certain effect of a shimmering background or some such ethereal sound. "It's too heavy and dull, strings; you know what I want—'Extase colour!'"

Nothing suits him so well as music built on his own scale —'The Ring', for instance, where the great phrases are made to mount towering heights as though in the hands of Wotan himself. After a vocal episode, when he has been keeping the orchestra restrained for accompanying, Coates with something like a whoop will burst out: "Now you can let go. This is *ours!*" And double *fortes* become double fifties! Yet he is capable of exquisite tenderness and extreme delicacy. Indeed, Coates is a man of immense range. Half-tones and half-measures are not found in him;

that intensely vital temperament needs everything or the least possible, glorious colours and extreme delicacy. Careful shading and detail are secondary to power and essential outlines.

He conducts a great deal from an extremely sound memory, which covers a large repertory and enables him to obtain a particularly close contact with the players. He has one curious scheme of rehearsing a new work. Having played it through, possibly with strings only, he will then take the wind and ask for one desk of the string department to remain—an unhappy skeleton. No music he plays will ever be dull. Everything will be intensely alive, and shot through with emotion and fire; and all hampering restraint cast aside.

EUGENE GOOSSENS
JOHN BARBIROLLI
LESLIE HEWARD
JULIUS HARRISON

EUGENE GOOSSENS

EUGENE GOOSSENS is a brilliant musician whose native country has been unable to retain his services. It is lamentable that the orchestral activities of Britain are so restricted. As things are, the lure of America has captured Goossens, to our loss. Outstandingly gifted in every way, he is one of the first musicians of his generation.

He began his career as a violinist, and for the Philharmonic String Quartet, of which he was a member, he wrote some of his most attractive music. There is no better training for a conductor's career than to have had some years' experience of playing in a first-rate quartet. It gives him that complete understanding and control of his strings which no conductor who is not a string player can quite achieve; and moreover, a thorough grasp of the art of ensemble, balance and intonation.

Goossens is blessed with a personality that sets him apart from the ordinary run of people. It is composed of charm, distinction, a kind of aristocratic youthfulness. He exercises an irresistible attraction over the players. And though the years go by, Goossens, with his slim figure and grace of gesture, cannot be thought of but as ever young.

His face, with its high forehead and pallor, is typical of the whole brilliant family. All of them have that high forehead, compelling eyes and rather sharp up-tilted nose. He speaks nowadays with a little American twang. The voice is clear, the enunciation admirable. Whatever he has to say goes quickly home to every player, and he never opens his mouth unnecessarily. Rehearsals are always smooth and tightly run—never slack or haphazard. But he never slogs or overdrives. He understands thoroughly the business of saving up for the concert, and he himself generates far more electricity and power when it comes to the night.

Close detailed work is not a feature of his rehearsing. He is not fussy or fidgety, though sharply critical of all technical shortcomings. "Gentlemen, you are not playing in tune; it sounds most objectionable. Oboe, please give them another A."

All his movements have the fascination of grace without effeminacy. America, which seems to spoil so many artists, has done him no harm so far as the orchestra can see, but has only added to his admirable self-confidence and polish. He has developed all his natural talents as a musician and conductor without the mannerisms or the exaggerated sense of self-importance which success in America has not seldom been known to entail.

JOHN BARBIROLLI, who dramatically sprang into the place of fame, was, to begin with, a 'cellist. Again, chamber music served this artist well; and he has carried his extensive knowledge of string playing even farther than Goossens, who rarely becomes technical in rehearsing string passages, leaving much for the leader to arrange, while Barbirolli edits his scores with complete bowing directions, and makes a point of insisting upon their observance. He has a habit of punctuating his remarks with a questioning grunt, the nearest rendering of which is "Eugh".

"I've never heard anything like it! Can't you play at the point of the bow, eugh? What's the matter? I've already asked you three times to play it at the point, and some of you are still sawing away at the middle, *eugh*! Now, don't let's have any more of this nonsense, please!" Smack of the baton on the desk, emphasizing his irritation.

His youthful and fresh-looking face, with his shock of dark hair, belies his great experience. Unlike Goossens he gives great attention to close detail, making his rehearsals very exacting and strenuous. He tackles a Haydn symphony in much the same way as Beecham, taking exquisite care with every phrase, and insisting that the strings play with unanimous detail in bowing and colour—like a quartet, in fact, and with the same polish. Intonation throughout the orchestra is the object of unremitting attention.

Much of his early work consisted of conducting opera. Not till he took over the Scottish Orchestra did he build up his reputation as a fine symphonic conductor. He is a tremendously hard worker, and his deep knowledge will always be equal to the demands made of it. He frequently conducts from memory. A story is told that he was performing a new work by Arnold Bax at an important concert and lost the score before the last rehearsal. He conducted both rehearsal and concert, with complete confidence, from memory. The orchestra has a vivid impression of his personality. A mature head full of experience and confidence, set on young shoulders! Very short in stature, he is also not unlike Napoleon in countenance. The orchestra has often wondered quietly what he would look like in a cocked hat. On the rostrum he has something of the grand and intolerant manner with which Bonaparte must have impressed his troops. The honour that has fallen to him of succeeding to Toscanini's post in New York is testimony to the vitality of the man and also to the musical life of his native land.

LESLIE HEWARD, the conductor of the Birmingham Municipal Orchestra, is not yet sufficiently recognized in London. Here is another brilliantly gifted musician capable of filling any big position as a conductor. Trained in Manchester as an organist, he turned to the pianoforte and quickly showed a natural brilliance, not only in performance but also in his amazing and apparently instantaneous grasp of a new score. His is no superficial assimilation; his mind goes deep into the meaning of the music, with unerring penetration. He wields an unmistakably clear stick, every movement of which tells—it is, in fact, one of the finest there is anywhere. Heward is a man who can obtain a first-rate result from scanty rehearsals; yet with an adequate time allowance he has plenty to say. He is blessed with a fine musicianship to which anything in bad taste is inadmissible. No music shows him up to finer advantage than Sibelius. It is a wholly satisfying experience to play any of that composer's major works under his baton. All his classical readings are sound, and the sincere and gifted musician in him is never overshadowed by the conductor. His accompanying is beautifully accomplished. Heward is one of those rare and sensitive artists who delight any soloist fortunate enough to play with him.

JULIUS HARRISON, conductor of the Hastings Municipal Orchestra, is one of those musicians of the more reflective type, who enjoy making music with the orchestra, rather than the glaring limelight of the virtuoso conductor. In addition to his great gifts and reputation as a composer, he was trained as a violinist in the early part of his career, and his useful knowledge of string playing is apparent in his rehearsals.

Harrison believes a great deal in thorough preparation before he comes to rehearsal—not only are his scores studied with great care, but he spends much time checking his orchestral parts; bowing all the strings, and giving full indications of any particular phrasing, and breath-taking for the wind. If any slight departure from the score is intended, then it will be all duly set down in the parts beforehand, to avoid unnecessary waste of time.

He is of the gentler order of conductors who depend upon a very quiet voice and intimate manner in his work with the orchestra. He is far removed from those dominating personalities who are for ever demanding this and that—instead, he appeals to the intelligence and artistry of his players. He can become as importunate as the Biblical widow if these virtues are not forthcoming; but he never plays the autocrat. Being an extremely sensitive musician himself, he expects as much from the players. He loathes anything blatant or vulgar, whether in the playing or in the music itself: his programmes will seldom include any work that does not conform to his high artistic standard. He shows much consideration for the orchestra and is quick to sense its health, he does not blindly break its spirit by unnecessary repetitions and an incessant demand for the utmost vigour.

"Gentlemen, I hear you have had a rather strenuous time in the last day or two, so to save ourselves unnecessary energy, let us look through this movement of the Dvořák symphony, as there are one or two difficult spots I should like to warn you about. At letter F, my experience is that the tone of the strings is apt to slip up where the brass enter; on the contrary—I want it still more sonorous.

"One outstanding figure, Lā-dā-pom-pom-pā—play it very distinctly every time you have it—it often becomes blurred and lost in the general sound, unless you drive it home with heavy staccato.

"Letter M. Don't hurry, strings, take plenty of time for that passage.

"Horns, your figure a few bars after letter Q sounds nicer if you lift the crotchets a bit.—Don't run them into each other as the tendency has it.

"Tuba, at that passage near the end of the movement; I want you to take the bung out!"

He always uses a quiet voice to address the orchestra, and does not raise it in anger whatever the circumstances. Intonation is one of his chief cares and he will patiently tackle it, however elusive the creature. He is often found in the middle of the orchestra, conducting a troublesome progression of chords in the woodwind, turning the handles himself, as it were, to correct the pitch. If a question is asked by any player about a doubtful note, Harrison will frequently step down from the rostrum to look at the part himself, instead of consulting the score. If a question of bowing appears in the string department, he generally has very decided opinions on the matter himself, and will walk up to the leader to discuss it for a moment or two. He never carries on a conversation from the rostrum.

When he stops the orchestra to say something, or sing a phrase, he has the habit of laying his stick down on the desk, detaching himself from the 'conductor' so to speak; he never waves it about or gesticulates unless he is actually conducting; unlike some other conductors. Mengelberg, for instance, never lays it down at all. If he is holding forth, the baton will be perpetually hitting or scraping the stand, for emphasis.

Harrison is measured in his speech—whatever he has to say will be after due thought, and not for the pleasure of hearing his voice. He sings a great deal to illustrate his meaning—and especially rhythmical figures—"Pōm-tĭddlĕy-ūm-tĭddlĕyūm-pŏm-pā—I want a very brilliant rhythm here, gentlemen. Going on!"

The whole essence of Harrison's work as a conductor is his enjoyment of music for music's sake, and most of the points in his rehearsing are to do with phrasing, balance and intonation, and a natural style of playing. His aim, to let the music speak for itself. He does not come before the orchestra to discourse or to bring some wonderful new interpretation, neither does he enounce dogmatic ideas and principles from an unassailable throne, but on the contrary, he makes music sitting in the midst of the orchestra, as it were: with patience and quietness as the cardinal virtues in the art of rehearsing.

SIR HAMILTON HARTY

SIR HAMILTON HARTY

SIR HAMILTON HARTY was a brilliant pianist and accompanist before he found for his poetic genius the way to the greater possibilities opened up by the art of conducting.

As a pianist he is renowned for his delicacy of touch as much as for his brilliance in execution, and his hand is no less delicate with the orchestra. He is an exquisite musician, full of imagination and spontaneity, and with the wayward spirit of the true virtuoso.

Intimacy with his orchestra is one of his characteristics; and only those who in his Manchester days worked with him in the Hallé Orchestra are really fitted to tell of this vital aspect of his life as a conductor. Many conductors do not need intimate acquaintance with their players and can achieve their finest results while remaining aloof from all personal contact, but Harty is one of those who wish to know their men. Cases are remembered in which he seemed to exercise something like a Svengalian influence over a player, giving him a sense of artistry that he was not able or willing to put forth for any other conductor. The astonishing success of the Hallé Orchestra when he was at Manchester must have been largely due to his personal sway over its members. This is a different thing from the magnetism a strange conductor can exert over an orchestra, being much nearer to the relationship of a wise parent to a family.

In all his orchestra training, his hand is never heavy or iron-fisted, but almost feminine in its light but exceedingly firm touch. He never employs a brutal manner or treatment in putting a matter right, but gently insists upon it without any strong words or temper. In the quietest of voices he will say:

"Now, boys, we must get this right. . . . No, it's not good enough yet. Let's try it once more; don't rush at it, take it in your stride."

A quiet voice is characteristic. In no circumstances will he raise his voice, even though he may have two or three extra brass bands scattered about the hall, as in Berlioz's 'Requiem'. If people cannot hear, then it's "their own fault for making so much noise" . . . He no doubt finds he can ensure silence in the orchestra in this way; though sometimes it is difficult for the players some distance from him to hear all he says. But the real reason for his quiet voice lies in his desire for an atmosphere of intimacy at rehearsal. Big as the orchestral work in hand may be, it is still for him something in the nature of chamber music.

He has an acute psychological knowledge of orchestral players, and relies on gaining their interest more than upon discipline. All Harty rehearsals are interesting, and rigid Germanic discipline is not for ever demanded, though he does not tolerate slackness or inefficiency of any kind.

He thoroughly understands the English temperament and the propensity to keep a little in reserve for the concert, and consequently does not drive "all out" at his rehearsals. Neither does he over-rehearse, nor ever make the orchestra practise anything unnecessarily. Great importance is

attached to "listening to one another," and to the understanding of the work by the whole orchestra. His players
are all separate human entities, not merely cogs in a machine.
In all the works he plays he tries to help a general understanding of the music; even at times giving the orchestra
a fanciful or poetic description, if he finds that to be the
clearest way in which to express himself.

"Boys, I think the composer had in his mind the picture
of a great gathering of people; the restless figure in the strings
represents the uneasy murmuring and confused sounds one
would hear with such a crowd.—I want you to get that
atmosphere into this music, as if you were there yourselves."

Many of his privileged artists he called by their Christian
names. With most conductors such familiarities would be
dangerous, but Harty is an exception. His use of Christian
names is typical of the intimate way in which he works.

"Archie, I want you to play this with complete freedom,
yet it must not upset the rhythmic figures in the accompaniment too much. Just play it with me by yourself, and I
will show you what I mean.—Yes, that's very good, but I
think it would be still better if you stayed on your top F
just a little longer, and then hurried the next passage slightly.
—I can keep the accompaniment going better.—Now, once
more.—Yes, that's first rate. Now, my dears, we'll do it all
together from the bassoon tune at letter B.—Archie, just
one more thing before we leave it.—Can you take breath
after the C sharp instead of in the bar before?—Good.—I
won't try it again now, it will be all right."

No conductor grants his soloists in the orchestra more

freedom for self-expression, though he will guide them and perhaps suggest different phrasings and other minor details. At the same time, he sees to the most subtle accompanying by the rest of the orchestra.

He has a genius for accompanying. This was apparent early in his musical career, when he made his name as a pianist. Harty as a pianist was a magnificent accompanist, and so he is as a conductor. In a concerto there can be none to surpass him. Not only does he give a wonderful support, but he also possesses the rare gift of intuition which enables him to anticipate the soloist's very thoughts. He may have acquired much by experience, but this gift was born in him, like his sense of poetry.

The orchestra is always conscious that it can play naturally and easily, without undue restraint or over-anxiety. He uses his stick with a characteristic economy of effort. Loosely held, it is most flexible and clear; and though the movement is graceful, the curves are never vague. Nor does the orchestra have to watch it too closely. All the time it is "just there," giving unmistakable indications.

Harty is extremely quiet in his movements. There is never an exaggeration of any kind in his gestures. In a wild passage his face becomes suffused with emotion, and without any great movement he obtains a terrific response from the players. He is fortunate in complete unselfconscious expression of his feelings. Nothing comes between him and the music he performs. Electricity he seems to be able to generate at will. One moment his sense of repose will fine everything down to the utmost tranquillity; then in a flash he can change the scene to one of wild orgy.

Berlioz's violent changes of mood are never more brilliant and vital than with Harty.

In none of his interpretations does he favour the mono-chrome. Colours are always in evidence. Harty's conduct-ing is extremely human. Not confined by the bonds of purism, he interprets his scores exactly as he feels. There is consequently a strong personal element in all his work. Were he not such a magnificent musician, criticism might say that he flavours his interpretations too much with his own personality. He does not insist on the meticulous following of every detail in the score, but reads a great deal between the lines.

But if any performance of his will be unmistakably "Harty", it will, at the same time, be supremely musical and artistic.

He has a quick wit, and there are stories that show he can be mordant. A distinguished foreign pianist, who had been reported as having made disparaging remarks on music-making in this country, appeared at a Hallé concert and missed an important entry. Sir Hamilton and the orchestra cleverly covered this up, vamping a couple of bars until the great man found himself again. After the concert, he expressed great satisfaction with the orchestra, saying it was nearly as good as the Berlin Philharmonic.

Like a flash, "On the contrary it is better!" came from Harty. The pianist was nonplussed. "I do not understand, Sir Hamilton. How can it be better than the Berlin Phil-harmonic?"

"Oh, yes, it is," said Harty, "it plays two more bars in the finale of your concerto."

Harty is a conductor the orchestra likes to serve, both at concert and rehearsal. This is not too common. Celebrated conductors generally have a habit of making each rehearsal a concert in itself, or perhaps worrying the players unduly with a wealth of detail. Harty makes his rehearsals, though quite intense enough for the purpose, interesting and happy affairs; and the concerts will be exciting and full of verve.

SERGEI KOUSSEVITSKY

SERGEI KOUSSEVITSKY

TO possess a great reputation as an instrumental virtuoso means a long start for a conductor when he confronts an orchestra. The effect is that the players are all put on their mettle—and not only those of his particular department. Throughout the orchestra all immediately seek to demonstrate beyond a doubt their mastery of their instruments.

Sergei Koussevitsky is a virtuoso. (Understand the word in the finest sense, a sense implying the service of brilliant technical accomplishments to the cause of art.) As a double-bass player he built up an international reputation at an early age. Later on he became a virtuoso of the orchestra. Through experience gained in many countries and culminating in his work with the Boston Orchestra—whose chief he has been since 1924—he has arrived at an exhaustive knowledge of the resources and possibilities of every orchestral instrument. And from one and all he demands the same mastery that he himself attained on the bass. He goes to any length to obtain it.

His personality is made up of typically Russian elements —nervous intensity and fire, a tremendous energy that is tempered by charm and humour, and withal something of a tyrant, a tyrant who must be constantly beguiled by the finest playing if he is to be kept within bounds.

Seemingly it is his custom to play the boundless tyrant from time to time. A day comes when the safety valve must be released, and the most innocent member of the orchestra may experience the descent upon his head of a torrent of wrath. In America a luckless bass-clarinettist who, as it happened, was enjoying a few bars' rest was once singled out as the scapegoat.

"It is impossible, I cannot work like thees! You, you, Mr. X.! How dare you sit there? I weel ask you to go if I haf not your attention."

And so on; and a scapegoat he had to remain until the pressure became normal again.

A rehearsal of 'Le Sacre du Printemps' at Queen's Hall once broke down.

"Eet is impossible—I can no longer work with you! You haf no rhyt'm! I don' know why eet is, but there ees no rhyt'm in vat you do." Then, muttered as he passes the violins on the way out: "I am sorry, but I go!"

He was persuaded back out of the Paris express only just in time. And all this was merely because of a misunderstanding or a miscalculation in the rehearsal time-sheet. The orchestra was the scapegoat.

No slip is ever allowed to pass at a Koussevitsky rehearsal. Nothing less than the utmost concentration is required the whole time, and Koussevitsky's grip never relaxes. The interruption of a quite important question on some detail of bowing has been known to provoke:

"Do not spik! If you spik I go home!"

Some such remark is generally called forth by an unguarded murmur in the orchestra. And woe to the string leader who turns to give whispered instruction to his department! Professional inquirers of doubtful notes are quickly suppressed.

Intonation throughout the orchestra and matters of ensemble are worked at ceaselessly until they are correct. And then, sometimes, through sheer nerves, they go wrong again and have to be tackled at subsequent rehearsal.

The painful treatment of insisting on repetition upon repetition of some particularly nasty passage by one section of the orchestra, while the rest sit and look on, frequently produces nerves, and demoralization sets in. Some wretched wight perhaps gets his fingers tied up, and Koussevitsky, his face expressing utter contempt, shrugs his shoulders, bangs the desk with his stick and says: "I must do some work with you alone!" This brought the house down on an occasion when the victim was a one-note man.

But such are the various springs of his nature that in the thick of a time of stress a howling "domino" may quite possibly result in a good story told against himself—and at once the atmosphere changes and calm reigns.

Koussevitsky's attitude is essentially that of the great executant who refuses to approach the platform until his technique is flawless. Incessantly he strives after the most perfect playing, and he conveys the feeling that if only he can succeed in making the players reproduce perfectly his own idea the interpretation will be supremely right.

His stick is a fine instrument of artistry. His beat is straightforward, and he must be one of the few famous conductors who are in the habit of giving one or two unobtrusive introductory beats for difficult openings, like that of the scherzo of the 'Eroica'. It certainly ensures confidence in setting a new tempo.

His magnetism is largely conveyed by his face, which is extraordinarily expressive, lighting up instantly at any playing that touches him—and this is not infrequent—and again clouding as quickly.

"Y'know, I don' like it!" said in an intimate manner, is one of his happiest comments, which generally precedes a valuable suggestion as to the turn of a phrase—very different from the crash of his baton on the desk, like a pistol shot, with: "Stop! Absolutely chaotic!" followed by a lengthy pause and then a curtain lecture on the text, "Rhyt'm! There ees no rhyt'm at all! Not sufficient you play in time —I must have rhyt'm, otherwise, I cannot vork vith you!"

When deeply touched he can come out with a warmhearted "Vonnderval!" to those nearest him, which quite offsets his biting criticism.

Koussevitsky never, to begin with, plays through any considerable section of a work. Taking the 'Eroica' symphony, for instance, he starts by working on the first two chords, which have to be repeated again and again to obtain his required effect of terrific rage. The volume of string tone does not satisfy him until the attack and power in the short crotchet becomes electrifying. Then he begins practising at a slightly quicker tempo than usual the first subject.

He makes no points other than those directed in the score. The quest of vital rhythm provides most of the reasons for stoppages and corrections. It seems that the string-playing can never be short and sharp enough for him. Only after repeated demands for "De bow deep in the strings" does he find satisfaction.

The great *tutti* chords across the beat, shortly before the double bar, he actually directs, not indicating the rests at all. Then: "*Pianissimo* must always have substance and arrive to the audience! Vibrato! Always vibrato in *pianissimo*!" This of the phrase immediately after the double bar.

In the 'Funeral March' immense weight is placed on the ascending grace-notes in the double-basses, which he directs on the first beat. The tune is moulded exhaustively to obtain a lovely quality, full of substance in spite of extreme quietness. The rhythmic accompanying figures in the strings are touched upon. But with the *non troppo adagio* of the tempo he adopts in this movement few difficulties of ensemble arise.

The utmost *sostenuto* is repeatedly demanded in the subject of the fugato, and a powerful rhythm in the semiquavers. A great, sustained sound, a lovely *pianissimo* quality from the strings, and the fullest volume at the climax —these take up most of the time. And, permeating all the rehearsal, are the phrases one must for ever associate with Koussevitsky: "Zing! Alvays zing your phrases! Eet ees absolutely necessary. Ther ees no music without zingen!"

Giving out streams of energy, he demands every ounce of the orchestra, and it may be suspected that some of the performances at his rehearsals are finer than those of the concert itself. Certainly few if any peaks are attained at the concert that have not been scaled at the rehearsal. The concert itself is less of a strain, for the conductor changes from being an insatiable refiner to the role of irresistible leader. A slip or even a bad mistake never seems to upset him at the concert. He either overlooks the matter or only betrays by a severe glance under raised eyebrows that his concentration has been distracted.

Gustav Holst used to tell of a marvellous performance at Boston of Wagner's 'Faust' overture, marred only by a glaring false entry by a bassoon—who stuck to his error. Holst half-expected the conductor to leap on his stand in fury, but Koussevitsky seemed not to move a muscle. It would have been a different story at a rehearsal!

With all his experience—as soloist as well as of conducting—he yet does not conduct from memory. He may but glance at the score, but it is always there on the stand. No conductor has a greater knowledge of the capabilities of an orchestra, and, since he also has the precious gift of communicating his mind, to work with Koussevitsky is an unforgettable experience which no player can fail to treasure —doubly so if he has had the advantage of half an hour or so of intimate study with him. A virtuoso of the orchestra, Koussevitsky is also an inspiration.

WILLEM MENGELBERG

WILLEM MENGELBERG

WILLEM MENGELBERG is one of those great virtuoso conductors who come to this country with an almost legendary reputation for training and handling an orchestra. And it takes a very short time to find out that his reputation is no mere legend!

Similar to Koussevitsky in his amazing skill and mastery of the orchestra, as in his outlook on music, he is of a more rugged nature and does not go to the extreme of his Russian counterpart.

Short in stature, inclined to be stout, with small features set in a large head, and a mass of red hair that stands up like a halo, he makes a first impression of fierceness; but when his face relaxes in a genial grin fancy will not be denied the thought of another Mengelberg who might have been a marvellous clown. This is irresistible when he indulges in the histrionic art and, striking an attitude, he declaims, "Zis is der phrase of an Olympic Mann!" After a sound that displeases him, he will purse up all his features, and produce a delicious grimace, worthy of Grock himself. This sense of humour dispels the somewhat uncompromising expression at first apparent. At rehearsal he removes his coat, revealing a long waistcoat with seven buttons.

He looks robust and his face is young for his age, which he says is "nearly eighty"; and his vitality throughout his rehearsals never flags for a moment, though he drives himself hard the whole time. When it comes to the concert he becomes a geyser of energy. His eyes are then compelling —or repelling if he takes a dislike to any one, and he has the trick of taking in every player individually. His magnetism comes from the man's whole personality. He seems to increase in stature upon the rostrum. And his will is felt, rather than seen. His baton, which is often dispensed with (on account, as he says, of an irritating corn) is used as a time-beater only, and for indicating rhythmic impulse; it is quite independent of his left hand, which is responsible for the entire range of expression and for balance.

He goes to pains to explain his left-hand gestures, a trait unusual in conductors who generally take it for granted that every gesture they make is absolutely unmistakable. When he wishes a certain solo to stand out he points with his first and second finger at the player concerned, and the rest of the orchestra must immediately give way. If the accompaniment is still too loud, he continues to point until the balance is correct. He does not, if he can possibly avoid it, make a gesture of restraint. The accompanying section of the orchestra has to understand that without his aid.

Such a wealth of detail is studied at rehearsal that he does not expect any trouble in balance at the concert. His hand then is generally concerned in directing the curve of the music and imbuing it with life and character. When a string passage is to be played with the utmost warmth and emotion he will curve his left arm up, as if he were a violinist at the great climax of a concerto holding his instrument as in ecstasy; and if it is a tune for any one of the three upper strings, he likes them to raise their instruments a little higher than is normal. "Ysayeissimo," he exclaims. In a great climax this gesture of extra effort is also required of the brass—horns, trumpets and trombones being directed to raise their instruments over the top of their stands.

His left hand may appear rather hard and unyielding but can none the less be made wonderfully sensitive and is capable of inspiring the most exquisite tenderness; witness the last episode of 'Heldenleben', which in his hands must be matchless for sheer beauty.

He rarely singles out any player for especial praise and is sparing with compliments of any kind. Yet at the concert he will let a "bravo!" escape him, which has a real sincerity behind it and is encouraging at a moment of strain. There can be a great kindliness in his rugged face, and though it does not always appear, it makes him very human. In former days, it is said that he ruled his orchestras with a rod of iron. With the years has come a certain mellowness, though he remains intolerant as before of any playing less than perfect. Instead of instilling fear into the hearts of his victims, he now turns to the art of dissertation, which is a strong feature of his methods of rehearsal. He will talk for ten minutes on end, and one can imagine his own orchestra at Amsterdam quietly sitting with their instruments on their knees, waiting for the rain of words to stop. Orchestras that are not used to him are rather tried by continually having their instruments up, ready to play, only to be caught by a sudden change of subject instead of the attack for which they have been holding their breath. He will go on talking for quite a long time with both arms still raised in the air at the "ready." During such discourses his waistcoat buttons offer themselves for counting, the more so since there are seven of them instead of six.

These dissertations are full of sound matter, and they take far less toll of the precious energy of the orchestra than the incessant demands for white-hot playing made by such a conductor as Koussevitsky whose rehearsals are like a series of terrific concerts. The great drawback is the havoc Mengelberg makes of the time-table. Punctual in beginning rehearsal and in resuming at the end of the fifteen minutes interval, he ignores the other aspects of time. He stretches the hours like elastic, which nearly breaks by the end of the last rehearsal. Half an hour after the rehearsal should have come to an end, he finds still one more piece which he has not yet touched. Right through his rehearsals time is of no importance. He will spend an hour and a half upon the exposition of the first movement of a concerto, with the soloist scarcely playing a note; and, at a final rehearsal, when every minute is precious, will change a whole lay-out, and have a piano and harpsichord removed from the platform, in order to begin with the work he has in mind. This meant once that an unfortunate artist who was to play the harpsichord in a Vivaldi concerto had to rehearse his part sitting in the stalls without an instrument.

This little matter of time apart, his great experience enables him to solve every orchestral problem. In a difficult work like 'Heldenleben' he hears everything and sees at the same time; instantly puts his finger on a weak spot, and proceeds to clear it up without losing his temper; and never resorts to sarcasm, or the time-honoured remark that every other orchestra "plays this easily."

Not the least part of his success in getting results is due to the scrupulously marked parts he brings with him. Detailed as possible in bowing, phrasing, and breathing instructions, they are all admirably practical and there is a definite purpose behind every mark.

As far as the strings are concerned, he is very definite that solo playing and orchestral playing require two different styles, and the bowing is marked accordingly. Knowing to the finest point what will sound clear to the farthest member of the audience, he is not content with apparent clarity on the rostrum. He knows that a string passage which, played in a certain way, would be perfectly satisfactory on a solo violin, may when played by a group of twenty, sound muddy at the end of the hall. He knows exactly the kind of bow to be used with the greatest effect. He mostly avoids too much *legato* in the strings, for, he says, definition tends to be blurred—"it will sound quite *legato* enough if there is air between the strokes of the bow."

This brings us to his favourite manner of expressing blurred playing. In a very scornful and powerful voice he will exclaim "*Ter-der!*" with the accent on the first syllable, and at the same time he makes a horrible scraping on his desk with his baton. The correct sound he wants is then indicated by his rapping out sharply with the butt end of his stick. "Ti-ta-to!" is his opposite exclamation to "Ter-der!" standing for clear, incisive playing and attack. The orchestra soon gets used to this dreary "Ter-der!" and takes all possible pains to avoid its recurrence. The exclamation, with the attendant nerve-racking scrape, is inclined to put the players on edge—which is precisely what he wants.

Mengelberg's rehearsals all point to the concert—he does not rehearse for rehearsing's sake, though he may talk for talking's sake. His unremitting attention to technical details of every kind, as they arise, results in magnificent and confident playing, which it is doubtful whether any conductor can surpass. The orchestra is completely and always confident in him, for he appears never to do anything different on the night from what he has previously shown at rehearsals. There are conductors who ignore points they have repeatedly made at rehearsal and who may give a different beat in a place where the orchestra is expecting an especially clear lead. Mengelberg is not one of them. He is the complete master in every way, and leaves no doubt whatever of his intentions even in playing an unfamiliar and unrehearsed work—which is most unusual, for the conductor who is accustomed to adequate rehearsal is seldom at his ease when playing "on his verve."

A virtuoso conductor, on his first appearance in front of a strange orchestra, generally says "Impossible!" and straightway proceeds to completely change the whole lay-out. Mengelberg, however, does not always alter everything.

When he conducted the B.B.C. Orchestra for the first time, he bowed to the exigencies of broadcasting, and only grumbled a little at having his basses and 'celli separated. He also likes his principal wood-wind in the centre, and the four horns the other way about to the usual procedure in this country, with his first horn in the centre of the orchestra. One or two minor changes were made in the brass, but nothing serious. He began by talking of the wonderful experiences he has had all over the world conducting every orchestra of note, for nearly fifty years, finishing with the remark, "And, you see, ther ees nothing I don't know!— Zo," (with a benignant "God help you" grin) "give me now the A, Mr. Oboe!"

Tuning with him is a ceremony that may take anything from five minutes to (in extreme cases) two hours. The first violins are directed to take the A only from the oboe, followed by the 2nds, violas, 'celli and basses. The rest of the orchestra then tunes, starting with the flutes and ending with the tuba. Not until the whole orchestra has the A are the strings allowed to tune their other strings. The oboe officiates like a High Priest, and has to stand and turn in the direction of the department concerned, for the benefit of those far away, while Mengelberg, sitting like a Buddha on the rostrum, criticizes the slightest deviation in pitch. On the first occasion this tuning took twenty-five minutes, and gave rise to his first dissertation:

"Eet has taken twenty-five minutes to tune—it should take two minutes! Der rehearsal, it begin wid tuning—eet ees no good, unless you are in tune! You may be first-class orchestra, but if you play not in tune?—It is difficult now for musicians—fifty years ago it did not matter so much perhaps; but now, it is necessary to haf full haus, and if you play not in tune, vell? Der haus, it will be empty! Der feerst oboe, feerst clarinet moost help deir colleagues, like a mutter her children; and, you, Mr. Oboe, moost make the face, if someone play bad A!—You moost vatch, like der cat der mouse.—There—dat leetle double bass, you hear heem behind there?"

Tuning eventually comes down to a matter of five or six minutes. If he is starting the programme with 'A Midsummer Night's Dream,' he will have all the wood-wind chords played to him at the last moment, before going on the platform.

Usually he likes five rehearsals for a symphony concert; two for the wind, two for the strings, and the final rehearsal together. He does not find it necessary to have more than one general rehearsal, for he says that if sufficient detailed work is put in by the two halves of the orchestra, he has no difficulty in joining them up.

Mostly he rehearses from memory.

The whole of his first rehearsal with the B.B.C. Orchestra was devoted to the opening portion of 'Heldenleben' as far as the entry of the solo violin.

Thoroughly characteristic of his methods was the way in which he tackled the great opening phrase. Each note of the arpeggio had to be detached, in spite of the composer's direction, because, he said, the audience should hear every note, "and if they are all slurred by the strings, there will be no definition, and the passage will only sound like a chord of E flat," whereas he wants it to make the effect of a brilliantly clear arpeggio. The first two notes after the tied minim are invariably lost in performance, consequently he puts a rest or comma in place of the tie. For the same reason he places another in the 2nd bar, after the dotted minim C, to ensure an incisive attack on the last beat of the bar, and the strings are directed to hit the E flat with the point of the bow. However, the next phrase is played *legatissimo* to the last beat of bar 4, in front of which a breath-mark allows for another attack leading to the two heavily accented minims.

Four bars before Fig. 1, he again cuts out the ties and inserts rests. This may, on paper, seem very drastic, but the effect in playing is brilliant; and the sharp contrast of *sostenuto* and *staccato* stands out with the greatest effect. Not only is this opening passage typical of his genius for producing superb playing, but it also shows his attitude to the composition he is interpreting. Nothing will induce him to obey blindly the composer's directions if his own experience tells him that they could be made more effective by a slight alteration. In his own words:—"Beethoven, like many other composers, sometimes made changements in his scores, even after publication, and then he also was deaf. So vy not the conductor also, who often knows mooch better than the composer? I vos de best pupil of Svhidler, who vos the best pupil of Beethoven, zo I know vat Beethoven meant. Zo, in dis verk of Strauss; I haf been great friend of Richard Strauss since I vos a boy, and I know joost what he wants, and ve vill make some changements also!"

He rehearses the opening as far as Fig. 2 at great length, first of all taking the violas, 'celli and horns, until there is complete unanimity in ensemble, phrasing, intonation and style, and all trace of untidiness at these inserted breath-gaps is removed. He arrives at the episode of the 'Critics' (1st bars before Fig. 14) after two hours' work, and makes the flute play his subject, *staccatissimo*, and as spitefully as he can, and the counter-subject in the oboe drawled and wooden, with each entry of the other wood-wind almost overblown in the anxiety to be heard. The celebrated

5ths of the two tubas are considerably broadened with a big *crescendo* and *diminuendo* to the held note. So much are they elongated that the rest of the orchestra has to adjust its playing to them.

He spent a long time at each rehearsal over this tuba motif. "Zis motif represents one of Strauss's most hated critics, M. Quentin, und eet moost sound like MONSIEUR QUENTIN. Play it to me!—No, it is not together! Boot you don't give me the *crescendo* to the second beat and then *diminuendo*! Now fur der last time!"

He rehearses all the first part of this section until all the contrapuntal parts are clear in every detail, and the utmost character portrayed in the different themes. At the end of this episode for wind he finds the accompaniment too heavy at the *pianissimo* syncopated chords in bassoons and horns, and later in the strings as well, so it gives him another opportunity to discourse on the playing of "accompaniments generally."

"You moost play with joost the right amount of tone, neither too mooch, nor too little, if you play an accompaniment too soft, then it ees joost as wrong as playing too loud. Listen to the soloist. Then, if you arhe der soloist, you moost be heard, even if der mark es *pianissimo*. Zo, not forgotten dat if you are accompanying, play less than vhat you haf, und when you arhe de soloist, play a leetle more. Eet moost be a hundred per cent and not joost seventy-five per cent!"

At "Festes Zeitmass", two bars before Fig. 22, he plays the four-bar passage six or seven times until the rhythm is sufficiently accurate and *staccato*; with frequent interjections of "Ter-der!!" The unfortunate solo violin does not get an opportunity to set out on his difficult solo until well into the middle of the second rehearsal—a very trying experience—for each time the conductor arrives at his entry he stops him in mid-air, on his first C sharp, and returns to a figure some way back. Much the same thing happened in Brahms's B flat piano concerto. He would let the pianist play one chord in his opening solo, and then stop and start again, working at considerable length over the first *tutti*, stopping the pianist each time in his first stride.

The ensuing passage in 'Heldenleben' contains many difficulties for the orchestra as well as the exacting solo for the violin. The first one crops up in the 'celli, basses and bassoons at the end of the 5th bar of Fig. 23, and continues much in evidence throughout the whole of the accompaniment to the violin. This is the elusive semiquaver which always precedes the principal subject of this section. "TER-DER, I don't hier dhat 16th note—vhat do you call it—semiquaver! Put der bow on the string and separate the note from der next bar. Give me furst der 'celli—zo—now der double basses—again, eet ees difficult! Better! Now, der 1st and 2nd horn. You will haf to play louder, 2nd horn!— Now, 'celli, basses, mit 1st and 2nd horn. Ah ha! I begin to hear it at last, eet is no longer Ter-der and nearly eighty per cent. 'Celli and bass, use mo-ore *glissando!*"

About ten bars further on he practises the *pizzicato* chords in the 2nd violins for ensemble and intonation, both times the passage occurs, demanding a clear but quiet plucking of the string at right angles for a dry sound, and not along the string for a more sustained sound. At the end of the solo violin passage at Fig. 32, he has further trouble with the "semiquaver" and does not continue until 'celli, basses, oboes, clarinets and bassoons articulate the note distinctly before the great G flat chord.

The next section might almost be labelled the "left hand of the strings", so frequently does he demand the utmost warmth and life in the vibrato, as much as in great breadth of bowing. He continues to take all those playing the same phrases in unisons and octaves separately, and often one department at a time, aiming at a rich and glowing sound where perfect intonation and ensemble increase the volume. Not until he obtains the right volume given him by these two matters—"one hundred per cent—and not joost seventy per cent!"—does he turn to the balancing of the parts.

Four bars after Fig. 38, he makes the utmost of the 1st and 2nd violin passage in octaves, by getting both departments to take the same amount of bow in exactly the same style and position, stopping instantly if any player is taking obviously too much or playing in the wrong part of the bow. "It ees no goot, dhat long bow in de orchester, it looks well, yes in der front, but de notes are not dhere! A soloist may do it perhaps, but eet ees no goot in der orchester."

At the trumpet call at Fig. 42 he insists on the absolute clarity of the first two notes of each part, even if it means making them longer than demi-semiquavers; clear articulation is more important than anything else here. Also the balance between the three trumpets must be equal. Immediately after this figure, he asks the basses and 'celli almost to "crush" the *sforza* on the B flat. "It is bad to crush ze tone, perhaps, boot hiere it is an exception! Yes,—I want it brutal" (and makes a fearful grimace).

He does not spend much time on the battle scene, and only insists that those tunes which stand out from the general din be clearly and accurately handled. The insistent rhythm which appears on the strings and side-drum at the "Festes Zeitmass" after Fig. 49 is hammered out as hard as possible, with short little jabbing strokes of the bow, near the heel; and drum and strings have to clear up a ragged ensemble, the side-drum being a long distance away. At the climax, two bars after 75 he again insists on the perfect articulation of the quaver—two semiquaver figure.

The tuba figure again fails to satisfy him before Fig. 85, but the violas and 2nd clarinet fortunately get over their shaky bridge at Fig. 85 without disaster. A typical stroke of Mengelberg's comes out in the 'celli, a few bars further on, their last sextolet being drawn out in a *molto allargando* and *diminuendo*, making an exquisite sound with the bows ust brushing the string before falling at length on the G major chord.

He touches upon the various quotations from Strauss's earlier works in the next episode, particularly demanding a special effort from the horns in their 'Don Juan' motif. After Fig. 94, in the semiquaver passages, he makes a terrific effect from the strings, by forbidding too much bow, as near the heel as possible, so that he gets articulation and *staccato*, even at high speed. Should any player forget himself and let his bow trickle to the point, he shouts, "Vy do you play dhere? It is no goot; I haf tolt you, you are not playing as soloist—you are in der orchester." The player is then eyed for a few moments: "Now we moost do it again!"

For the last time, he makes sure of getting every semi-quaver clearly played after the tied notes, between Figs. 95 and 96, and at the end of the episode he takes the great descending quintuplet in two beats, making groups of two and three.

In the concluding scene, a Mengelberg of extreme gentleness appears, capable of exquisite tenderness; and the lovely interjectory phrases on the first and second violins, during the cor-anglais solo, are made to sound as if there was all humanity in them. The left hand of the violins is singled out for his medium of expression, the bows held well in control to avoid over-emphasis. The violin solo to the end is made to tell on every note, and the player is able to play with complete freedom, both in expression and delicacy, with the rest of the orchestra hushed to an extreme *pianissimo* which is yet alive—the colour of a moving part just coming to the surface now and again.

With all his dictatorial grip of his players, he seems to need a similar grip on the part of his soloists in the orchestra. If he senses that responsive grip his hand becomes like velvet and at the performance he will himself respond to the players' expression and bring it to full bloom. But if he cannot obtain what he wants from an artist, he will be hard as iron and may seem to oppose rather than aid. He has the true virtuoso's intolerance of inadequate playing; he expects to be able to start his rehearsing from scratch, without having to nurse any weakness amongst his players. His ear detects everything. His particular genius is for hearing from the point of view of the man at the back of the hall. Besides satisfying him, this redoubles the clarity for the rest of the audience.

His interpretations, intensely personal and vivid, have his great conviction behind them. Though he may depart from the directions of the composer, audience and orchestra alike are carried away by the grip and mastery of it all. He holds everyone close, and a whole department of strings will think that his eye is compelling each man individually.

An orchestra that is proud of its work and is without passengers can look forward to working with Mengelberg, as a student to a lesson with a great master. Each man knows that he will be able to put forth all his own skill and power to the utmost advantage under him, and enjoy the exhilaration of taking part in magnificent playing. It is good for an orchestra sometimes to show off all its skill for its own sake, and Mengelberg knows as much as any conductor living how to make this possible. Long dissertations at rehearsals may be more trying, but there is always some truth in what he says, and though the time-table may go wrong, his rehearsals really are rehearsals.

Mengelberg inspires an orchestra to its utmost power, and to sit under him is to sit at the feet of a great virtuoso. As he says, and it is most true, "There ees nothing I do not know about der orchester." An orchestra, having finished a rough passage with him, will have humming in their ears, like the sound of the sea in a shell: "Ter-der—hoondered per cent; Ter-der—hoondered per cent—always hoondered per cent."

MODERN MUSIC

MODERN MUSIC

FROM the point of view of the orchestra modern music can be (a) stimulating and thrilling; (b) interesting and increasingly intelligible, though laborious at rehearsals; or (c) dull, abominably difficult and possessing every disagreeable attribute but smell.

In the main, the orchestra is always interested in playable music, when the instruments are exploited and not frustrated. What it hates is having to plough through badly or perversely written stuff. Much of the music that Schönberg and his disciples are writing is exasperating to play. Instead of a few bars of genuine music for one's instrument, one is seldom allotted more than a group of two or three notes, and these are generally separated by complicated rests. Even a whole department of the orchestra will not often get more than a quarter of a phrase to play, and the notes themselves are scored over with a multitude of complicated directions almost impossible to carry out. It is common to meet in Schönberg or Alban Berg with a single bar of eight quavers over each of which there is a different indication. Such a bar is simple in that it has no rests or complicated time-values, but the example will give an indication of the hair-splitting characteristic of the Schönbergian school.

And after all the only people who make any endeavour to observe these marks are one or two specializing conductors! One such used to get so hot and bothered that he invariably wore an umpire's white-linen coat to catch the perspiration which after a minute or two dripped from him, and his magnifying glasses needed a form of screen-wiper to deal with the moisture, while an armful of towels was never really adequate. With the most painstaking Teutonic patience he did his best faithfully to follow the composer's directions, to the utter distraction of the orchestra; but when it came to the night, nothing seemed to matter very much, and all the hair-splitting went by the board.

After the sea of perplexity in the new Viennese school, Hindemith is easy game. A player himself, he writes extremely playable music, some of which, especially of his later period, like the 'Mathis' symphony, is enormously interesting to play. And then, Hindemith is so wholly efficient and delightful a conductor to work with that there is never the slightest fuss, and the difficulties his work entails are met more than half-way by his good humour and equanimity. His beat is very clear, without any frills, and he might be chewing the cud of reflection, so calm and collected is he in the complicated pages of his scores.

Prokovieff is a faithful portrait of his music, which is uncompromising, steel hard in its precise rhythm and bare lines but rich in humour and satire. His manner is downright and clear-cut; and his mind quick to sense every happening, particularly that which is not entirely to his liking. His gestures are economical and clear as his scoring, while angular and without the slickness and technical facility of the conductor proper. He shows no feeling whatsoever; nor does he at any time ask for great expression—a singular characteristic in a Russian, for Russian conductors can as a rule never be satisfied with the orchestra's emotional response.

Prokovieff looks a great deal at his scores, though if necessary his eyes immediately glance at the player concerned; they are not chained to the music. He is wonderfully quick in grasping every position in the orchestra, however unaccustomed he may be to it, and he never, even in the first few minutes of his rehearsal, hesitates for a moment. On being introduced to the orchestra, unlike most composers, who generally ask a few questions or seek out the first player of each department, or possibly say a word or two in preparation, Prokovieff instantly raises his stick to begin playing. After the first few chords of his 'Romeo and Juliet' ballet he immediately stopped the orchestra and in a powerful voice demanded:

"Trombones, you will see that you are marked *forte*; but you must not play louder than the horns, who are also marked only *forte*. You play too loud now. Listen to the horns, and play with the same strength."

His conducting is rhythmical and clear, but uninspiring, and he does not stop a great deal for technical difficulties. Having cleared up a few wrong notes in the parts, and some made by the players, he wastes little time and quickly gives the orchestra a grasp of the essentials. His 'Classical Symphony', one of the most brilliant virtuoso pieces in the orchestral repertory, found him unexpectedly easy to please. Having had a lively time over this work with Koussevitsky, the orchestra expected some similar treatment, but the composer took it almost casually and at fairly easy *tempi*. He speaks excellent English, and gives the impression that he could write it even better. If it were not that humour saves him from cold inhumanity, he would seem to be a merely efficient robot. He is quick to seize upon any one who is not doing his job. The non-arrival of an important wood-wind solo suddenly roused him and the orchestra felt a shock as Prokovieff in an enormous voice indignantly roared:

"Good morning, good morning! You have an important solo there; why do you not play it? Mark it in red!"

This bass voice of his is like an amplified loud-speaker, and it suddenly woke up a talkative desk of fiddles, who were asked "to leave their club for a moment" and attend to business. No playing seems to touch him at all; provided that the orchestra is rhythmical, clear and in balance he has very little to say, unless to check a tendency here and there to hurry or drag.

"I have the idea that you have played this movement before at a quicker tempo. I do not like it any faster, and I must ask you to follow my beat and not try to push me."

It is curious that though he is always playing from memory as a pianist, he does not conduct from memory. At forty-seven, he is still remarkably youthful, and his arresting and autocratic personality, tall figure and head that might have been modelled by Epstein leave a strong impression upon the orchestra.

Kodály is a strange and striking figure. A man of fewer words never raised a stick; and he is extraordinarily restricted in his movements. Judged by the usual standards of stick technique he should be a poor conductor, yet he invariably obtains fine results. There are misunderstandings sometimes, particularly at the beginings of movements and after pauses, but they do not weigh much in the balance of the whole performance, which can be vital and powerful. The superficial impression the man gives is belied by his music, which is rich in colour and brilliance and bubbles over with spirits. Kodály is silent and aloof in his relations with the orchestra, only very occasionally giving them a wintry smile. He often conducts from a minute score of about the same size as a thumb prayer-book. His gesture is sometimes so inconspicuous that not long ago he had three shots before getting a movement to begin.

Bruckner's symphonies, it has to be confessed, are not looked upon kindly by English orchestras. Such protracted works are troublesome in rehearsal, and the strain becomes back-breaking. But, what is more, Bruckner is uninteresting to play. Mahler, on the other hand, can be delicious. Yet the endless sustained notes of the slow movement of his 4th symphony is dreaded by the strings. Only a string player knows what it means to play long sustained notes that must be kept alive with the left hand for about fifteen minutes on end. It is bad enough for the violas in the opening of the slow movement of Tchaikovsky's No. 5, to give a modest example of this *bête noire* of string playing. Only one thing is worse—*tremolando*—*fortissimo*—*in perpetuo!* Yet a curious phenomenon is the effect of just such devices in Sibelius.

Looking at any string part in Sibelius's symphonies, a

player might wilt with dismay. Nothing is there, apparently, but pages and pages of quasi-tremolando and sustained syncopated harmonies. But when one of these symphonies comes to rehearsal, under a conductor like Beecham or Koussevitsky, the music itself is powerful enough to grip the entire orchestra, whatever the lack of interest in the individual parts. Sibelius is unique in this way. Sibelius has only once or twice conducted in England, and that was many years ago. He was not then regarded as a first-class exponent of his own music. Few composers are able to resist the temptation to conduct. Arnold Bax is one of them and Alban Berg, it is said, rarely performed as a conductor. But almost the whole array of contemporary composers take their place on the rostrum at some time or another, and many of them are remarkably efficient.

Elgar in his later life conducted some things extremely well, though he was perhaps never quite first-rate. His command of the stick increased with his years, and though he did not overcome a certain woodenness and failed to accompany his concertos well, his variations and particularly 'Falstaff' and the 2nd Symphony were admirable under his direction. He had a great admiration for the orchestra and showed it in his attitude towards the players, who consequently did their utmost. Never was he seen to lose patience, and certainly never his dignity.

If dignity still means something, Elgar personified it in the great sense. There was never any affectation, and that grand figure facing the orchestra at a concert of his own works, near the end of his long journey, has left a picture that will never be dimmed in the minds of those present. One can still hear that vibrating, deep voice explaining at rehearsal some point in the music while he restlessly turned back the corners of the score. With a great urgency he would say, in a shaking voice: "Now, gentlemen, at this point (*scherzo*, Symphony No. 2) I want you to imagine that my music represents a man in a high fever. Some of you may know that dreadful beating that goes on in the brain—it seems to drive out every coherent thought. This hammering must gradually overwhelm everything. Percussion, you must give me all you are worth! I want you gradually to drown the rest of the orchestra."

He would never tire of telling the orchestra a story against himself of a performance of 'Gerontius.' He had been invited into the Lord Mayor's box, and was ushered to a seat next the great man, who had not caught Elgar's name on his introduction. After the first part the Mayor turned to Elgar: "What do you think of this music?" Taken aback, Elgar stammered some vague reply, whereupon the Mayor glared at him. "Young man, I think it's a horrible noise. I've never heard such nonsense!"

If a general opinion from the orchestra were asked, Elgar would be named as its favourite composer—certainly of any music written in the last forty years. He laid himself out to compose for the orchestra's joy, and often he would turn to the 2nd violins:

"Now, seconds, I want you to enjoy this passage. I wrote it specially for you!"

Is there any other music in the world so well calculated to delight any player as the Variations? And the Introduction and Allegro still reigns supreme above all music for the perfection of its string writing. The audience must recognize the orchestra's gratitude. Do we betray our loathing of music that is ill-written for the instruments? A full score may look a wonderful mosaic on paper. It may be fascinating to see the semblance of a tune divided up and down the orchestra, so that no instrument plays more than two consecutive notes of it. But heaven help the orchestra! Performance may be a nightmare of strain and misery.

Even a magical composition like Berg's opera 'Wozzeck' affords little pleasure to the executants, though it is not an extreme example of the school. Berg wrote music that the orchestra can understand as such, but as much cannot always be said of Schönberg and Webern. A rehearsal of some contemporary works comes to be dreaded like a visit to a torture chamber, what with the orchestra's attempts to interpret the general sense, and the attempts of a sub-interpreter to give us the gist of his exegesis.

One occasion is remembered when the score comprised among other things a harmonium, two guitars and a collection of such things as cow-bells, sheep-bells and brushes. After much argument the seating of the orchestra was arranged. The beginning of the work seemed vague, but it was not vague enough—everything was ordered to be more hushed. Then came a long discussion between the conductor and his interpreter, and after much consultation with the score and peering through magnifying glasses at the players, the recalcitrant instrument was at last discovered—the harmonium. This friendless thing had only one note to play, though several times and with a most complicated rhythm. This note could not be heard to the conductor's satisfaction, and every other instrument was instructed to let its *pianissimo* almost fade away. Still the desired sound eluded the conductor. Not until after much further argument was it discovered that the single note required of the harmonium was not available at all, something having gone wrong with the works.

Modern English music is grateful and comforting after this, and our composer-conductors are blessedly easy to understand after exasperating difficulties with foreign conductors who know little English and will not use an interpreter. The head of all our English music—Vaughan Williams—is a delight to any English orchestra. Something has already been said of a certain humility often seen in the truly great man. Not only is everyone conscious of this in our beloved Vaughan Williams, but he—in this unique in the entire realm of composers—cannot ever take himself at his full worth. The typical composer is naturally inclined to regard his own contribution as the most important work on the programme, and nothing is so rare as to find one who is detached and self-critical at rehearsal. Most are touchy if people are not taking an absorbed interest in them. But Vaughan Williams has been known to mutter of his own work, as he came off the rostrum: "Well, if that's modern music—I don't like it!"

Here is another example. A query arose about a certain note, and a player asked him if B flat was correct. Vaughan Williams searched the score, blinked at it, and with a rueful smile remarked: "Well, it looks wrong, and it sounds wrong—but it's right!"

As a conductor he is not a great technician, but few composers get such satisfactory performances of their own music. Young conductors please note: Vaughan Williams is a fine example of how a conductor should approach an orchestra. Calm and collected, he wastes no time but gets on good terms with the orchestra in about three words. Granted, this is easy for him because of the profound admiration the orchestra has for him both as man and musician. But that is the whole point. He has been years building up his great fame. Being where he is he can convey to the orchestra the sincere conviction he has that he has nothing in the least to be proud of, but that on the other hand, he is exceedingly proud of conducting us. He has the two most precious possessions of any conductor—great and sincere humility and a complete understanding of the minds of the players. His stick is clear enough for his needs, and though he may not give the impression of effortless ease in his movements and gestures, he stands fairly on his two adequate boots, and there is a grand solidity and structure about any performance he is directing. He can get anything he likes from an orchestra. Delicacy and swiftness are given him for the asking; the orchestra needs no subtle gestures from him. We understand everything he wants, and give it to him, full measure. What an orchestra asks for is a man it can admire, and Vaughan Williams stands for everything English we love.

His friend Gustav Holst received a similarly warm response whenever he conducted his own works. The two men were so closely associated throughout their lives that at Holst's death no one was more fitted than Vaughan Williams to talk of him. The following words made such a deep impression on the orchestra present when this talk was broadcast that with Dr. Vaughan Williams's consent they are included here:

I want to speak to you for a few minutes about the great composer, Gustav Holst, whose music you are to hear to-night.

Holst was a visionary but, at the same time, in all essentials a very practical man. He himself used to say that only second-rate artists were unbusinesslike. It is the blend of the visionary with the realist that gives Holst's music its distinctive character.

Besides being a composer he was a great teacher, a wonderful friend, a helper and counsellor to all who needed it. His teaching and his friendship we can no longer experience directly, but the works of art which are the connotations of a fine character are with us for ever and will, I firmly believe, be loved more and more as time goes on.

Holst's life gave the lie to the notion that a composer must shut himself away from his fellows and live in a world of dreams. Holst was, it is true, a dreamer—his whole nature, and the music which exemplifies his nature, seem to be hovering on the verge of an unseen world. But he never allowed his dreams to become incoherent or meandering. He loved life—in the best sense of the word—too much and he loved his fellow creatures too much to allow his message to them to appear in vague or incomprehensible terms.

Partly of necessity and partly from choice he lived in the common world of men. While he was still young, he was strongly attracted by the ideals of William Morris and, though in later years he discarded the medievalism of that teacher, the ideal of comradeship remained with him throughout his life. He wanted to work with and teach and to have the companionship of his fellow-beings.

His music is sometimes described as mystical, and rightly so, but we must not imagine from this something precious or vague. His texture, his form, his melody is always clear-cut and definite. Whenever he puts pen to paper, the signature Gustav Holst is clear to read in every bar of the music.

It is sometimes true of English composers that though they may have fine and poetical ideas, yet they lack that final power of realization which is a necessary part of a complete work of art. But it is emphatically not true of two English composers that we have lately lost, and I think for the same reason in both cases: namely, that Elgar and Holst learnt their craft not so much from books and in the study as from practical experience and from the nature of their material.

Already in his student days Holst had to eke out his meagre scholarship money by remunerative work, and he deliberately chose not to shut himself up in the organ loft or to give half-hearted pianoforte lessons to unwilling pupils, but to go out into the world armed with his trombone, earning his living where he could, playing now in a symphony orchestra, now in a dance-band, now in a Christmas pantomime at a suburban theatre. In later years came other activities, teaching and conducting. It was these experiences which gave him that grip of the facts of music which helped to build up his wonderful technique.

To many men this constant occupation with the practical side of music would have been a hindrance to inspiration, but to Holst it seemed to be an incentive. The fact that his creative work had often to be crowded into the short two months of a summer holiday gave him his great power of concentration and the intense will to evoke at all costs those thoughts that lay in the depths of his being.

Holst had no use for half-measures, whether in life or art. What he wanted to say he said forcibly and directly. He, like every other great composer, was not afraid of being obvious when the occasion demanded it—nor did he hesitate to be remote when remoteness expressed his purpose. But whether he gives us the familiar chords and straightforward tunes of 'Jupiter' or leads us to the farthest limits of harmony as in 'Neptune', his meaning is never in doubt—he has something to tell us that only he can say and he has found the only way of saying it.

Holst knew the orchestra even better than Vaughan Williams for he had played in one for many years and thus had greater inside knowledge of the works. Holst's music is the more exciting to play, and much of it demands brilliant virtuosity. Inside the orchestra one is very conscious that Vaughan Williams is deeply human and friendly in his music, while Holst seems to inhabit another world. Yet there is such power in Holst that a work like the 'Hymn of Jesus' still sends shudders down the back of the toughest players. And it is a choral work! 'The Planets,' 'The Perfect Fool' ballet, and many other compositions give as great a chance to the orchestra's resources of skill and artistry as any music ever written. As a conductor Holst was completely efficient and, in the latter part of his life, exacting. He was a fine critic of the orchestra and speedily found out the weak spots. But invariably he was charming and helpful, and he too had the virtue of humility. Praise from him was worth having. "I say, that was a grand show —couldn't have been better! My word, I've never heard anything in my life like that brass!—I must go and congratulate them."

Arnold Bax has endowed the orchestra with a magnificent library of works, all of them of great interest to play and many of them extremely difficult. Although he should not appear amongst composer-conductors, for he has never been known to conduct, so well-known a figure cannot be omitted. At rehearsals he is generally prowling round the back of the rostrum, aiding and abetting the conductor. Extraordinarily diffident and self-effacing, he never fusses the orchestra and he seldom changes his mind on his scoring, leaving all such matters to the conductor. The orchestra finds rehearsals trying when there are two minds in control, but Bax is generally only concerned with queries and matters of balance or *tempi*. He is never dictatorial, never touchy or irritable. Some composers—mostly foreign ones —get quickly upset and are impossible to please. Many of Bax's works, like 'The Garden of Fand', 'Tintagel' and the 3rd Symphony, are as thrilling to play as to listen to, while some, by reason of the peculiarity of the scoring, are difficult to hear inside without distortion. Bax has always held to his hard-and-fast rule NEVER TO CONDUCT. His scores, however, are so carefully edited that conductors are able to get a very clear idea of his mind.

To play unedited Delius, on the other hand, is like living in an empty house. Having heard Beecham perform his works, the composer must have realized it was hopeless to try to put on paper all that the conductor's intuition had read into his scores. Unless Beecham edits all Delius for posterity there will be a danger of this composer's music dying. Delius never seemed to know exactly what he wanted. A violinist once played a passage of his in three entirely different ways, asking the composer each time if that were what he meant. Each time came the reply—

"Yes." So in the orchestra, unless a conductor has great imagination, like Beecham, Delius can be appallingly dull and meaningless. Yet who can forget the glorious experience of playing a work like 'Eventyr' with Beecham? Works like the 'Cuckoo', and 'Summer Night', are now so well-known to the orchestra that they go with most conductors, but not so the lesser-known Delius.

Arthur Bliss and Constant Lambert share the honour of being the most efficient composer-conductors. Both are first-rate, with all the technique and experience necessary for the task their own music sets them. Dictatorial and military in manner, Bliss obtains cheerful, clear playing and, as he has superb confidence in himself, the orchestra is never at a loss. One of the most difficult passages of orchestral music ever written occurs in the middle of the 'Red' movement of Bliss's 'Colour Symphony', for wood-wind. But the composer never appears anxious, and always gives a perfect beat. He has the same clarity of mind and precision as the big conductors. There is never any doubt about his being in complete control of the whole performance, and his rehearsal will be conducted with clear and concise method. He is extremely critical, and tackles the orchestra in much the same fashion as an experienced orchestra trainer—not like a composer. His staccato, military voice emphasizes his authoritative bearing. His conducting serves his music brilliantly.

Constant Lambert is also completely master of his orchestra, he conducts other men's music as admirably as he does his own and possibly with more care. Less authoritative in manner than Bliss, he still has a strong grip and is extremely purposeful and definite about everything. He is not less clear and easy to follow than Bliss, but the two are dissimilar in method, Lambert being more imaginative in conception and less critical of execution. His ear is more than adequate and he always gets his way. A work of his composition receives no unduly favoured treatment at rehearsal, whatever its difficulty. His strong rhythmic sense and clear stick, together with his innate musicianship, make him a refreshing personality to the orchestra.

Frank Bridge, one of the finest masters of string playing in the country, has a great knowledge of the capabilities of the orchestra generally. He also conducts other music than his own and with the same understanding. He and John Barbirolli are our two distinguished conductors who have forsaken their instruments for the baton. Bridge was a first-rate viola player, especially in the field of chamber music. The outcome of this experience is that his music is delightful to play, especially in the string departments. He and Elgar are alone in being able to direct all the bowing of the string parts in their compositions, and in this respect Bridge is more expert even than Elgar, since his point of view is that of a really fine player. His chamber music is masterly in its colours and the aptitude of writing for the medium, and no less than his orchestral works it gives the player rare pleasure.

With this great knowledge he is naturally an exacting and extremely critical conductor. One wishes that he would demonstrate a phrase on his viola occasionally—as one repeatedly wishes for Casals to seize a 'cello—when asking for some particular effect.

William Walton restricts his appearances before an orchestra to performances of his own works, which he conducts with adequate skill and complete absence of fuss. Though his stick technique is probably not the result of any very intense application, it takes him through a maze of intricate bars—7/4, 15/8, 4/2, 3/8, 2/6, or whatever they may be—with the easy nonchalance of a guide discoursing on the places of interest from a charabanc. Pale of face but extremely calm, he never gets rattled. Not in the least dictatorial or fidgety over his own work, he is quite able to give an excellent performance, though he is not a conductor of the calibre of Lambert or Bliss.

John Ireland is not a good conductor, and his music is generally better served by another's direction of the performance. The orchestra, however, enjoys him on the rostrum, for he has a sense of humour and he puts himself in the players' hands. He frequently changes his mind about passages in his own works and, though they may have been played many times, the orchestra is never quite sure which version is correct. Even if he is not conducting, he will spend a long time retouching his scoring and phrasing from behind the rostrum. There is always fun when Sir Henry Wood is conducting an Ireland work, especially when pressed for time in the Promenade season. Ireland's music is rugged and powerful in effect and is well-written from the orchestra's point of view. His personality is almost inseparable from the music; even if he is not present, the orchestra waits for his voice shouting something to the conductor, who sometimes is patient, or, at other times, not.

Gordon Jacob is a remarkably efficient conductor of his own music and, rarely though the opportunity may occur, of other men's as well. He is one of those whose orchestra technique enables him to use profitably every moment of a rehearsal. Before he begins, every detail in the parts has been scrutinized and made unmistakably clear. Here is a composer who can give lessons to many of his more famous brethren in the matter of accurate scores and parts. His scoring is masterly and brilliant, and the first performance of a Jacob composition will be rehearsed in half the time that another's will want. He knows exactly what an orchestral part should look like, and personally sees that it is correct to the last iota. A leaf out of Sir Henry Wood's book! His conducting is characteristic of himself—a sturdy figure without any airs or graces, blunt but appreciative. He repeats nothing that does not need repeating. His music is always grateful to play, and the orchestra is able to hear every note.

Dame Ethel Smyth has a theory that if she had been a man her way as a composer would have been easier. What is more probable is that had she not been a woman, recognition would have come to her earlier and possibly more easily as a conductor. Women seem to be handicapped as conductors. They nearly all give the impression to the orchestra that it is as unnatural to them to wave a stick as to throw a cricket ball. Though grace is woman's attribute, few women conduct gracefully. Dame Ethel always gives a fine, clear beat, but it has at the same time a certain awkwardness. Vigour is a characteristic of all Dame Ethel's work, whether in composition or with the baton. The prelude 'On the Cliffs of Cornwall' stands out as a magnificent piece of music to play; and there is nothing she conducts better. Power and decision she has in abundance, and had she had a longer experience, ease and natural gesture must assuredly have been hers. She has that gift which is so desperately important for a conductor—great personality on the rostrum. Her lively humour and appreciative attitude make her rehearsals good-natured and very human occasions.

Dame Ethel cares less for detail than tor the spirit of the music in hand, especially when the spirit is jovial.

"Now, this march must be an extremely hearty affair. You should have heard the Suffragettes singing it at the top of their voices in Holloway Gaol. I used to conduct with a toothbrush from the top window.—That's the way I want you to play it!"

Another time, in 'The Bosun's Mate' she complained of the "Sunday School atmosphere." "But you must try to be a lot of drunken sailors! I want a great rollicking sound, and you can roll about in your chairs if you like! What I don't want to see is a lot of stuffed dummies!" The occasion is remembered when she suggested that the choir in 'Hey Nonny No!' should sway on their feet to the rhythm, but Sir Henry, who was there, did not think it very advisable. "We don't want any accidents!"

She has splendid assurance and is entirely unmoved by an audience. The orchestra will never forget her coming on to conduct at the Proms, dressed in a most impressive gown like an academic robe; and as she reached the rostrum, suddenly addressing the audience: "Ladies and gentlemen, I am sure you will be most interested to hear that this work will again be played in three weeks' time at the Leeds Festival." No one else in the world could do that—unless it were Sir Thomas.

Magnificently untroubled by what any one thinks, she is always completely herself. Pose or affectation of any kind is abhorrent to her, and what people think of her hats is not her concern. Dame Ethel is one of this country's greatest women. It is not forgotten that in the days of the Suffragettes she gave up her adored music completely for two years to help the cause which had struck her generous nature as deserving the sacrifice. The orchestra has always appreciated her true worth.

MALCOLM SARGENT

MALCOLM SARGENT

"GENTLEMEN, I don't want to worry you too much, but we must put all this beginning right. Clarinets, in that three-quaver figure, play the last one a little lighter than the others, but not so light as you made it—you don't hold it long enough. I want it just lă-tā-tă, lă-tā-tă, not lă-tā-tă, lă-tā-tă. It must not be short and staccato but played quite naturally, as if pronouncing an ordinary word of three syllables."

This is a typical opening of a Sargent rehearsal.

Malcolm Sargent has had a meteoric career. Setting out on his musical education he was articled as an organist to Dr. Keeton at Peterborough. Then he went to Melton Mowbray and his gift for choral conducting soon became talked about. Also he was a remarkable pianist—all this when he was barely out of his teens.

Soon he found himself conducting one of his own compositions at a Promenade Concert. A vivid memory remains of an extremely thin and wiry young man with flying arms, crashing with a breathless orchestra through 'Impressions of a Windy Day', as the piece was called. His stick moved so fast that it could scarcely be seen but seemed to make a blur like the spokes of a fast-moving wheel. And all the time he was rehearsing he never stopped talking.

He was like this in all his youthful activities—with choir, with orchestra, and with festival committees. And men looked at one another and asked, "Who is this extraordinary young man, who seems to know all the tricks of the trade and carries everyone along at the same breathless pace as his own?" "Can't any one stop him?" "I wonder how old he really is?"

Analysing this extraordinarily gifted personality, we find that nothing stands out more clearly than his amazing ability to assimilate anything he is studying. He has an uncanny way of mastering a score in about one-fifth of the time any one else would take over it, and he is like Sir Henry Wood in the way he imparts it to the orchestra. He is able to read it off to the orchestra just as an expert accompanist transposes a difficult accompaniment—faultlessly. His eyes are apparently not on the score, even if it is an entirely strange one, but, like lightning, always glancing at the players.

Lightning is the word to apply to him. It is inside him. Everything he does flashes quickly. He is never still—even if his body is motionless his looks will dart and miss nothing. His face is always animated; not only is he continuously looking at the players, but incessantly he clamours for an equal response.

"You know, gentlemen, I do not catch your eye. You look at the parts too much. I must have you looking at me more—we can't possibly get any ensemble otherwise. Some of you are very good in this way, but there are others who seem perfectly indifferent and just look glumly at their music. Now I must have your eye, gentlemen."

Never has any one seen him lifeless, though he has been afflicted with a serious illness; to the orchestra he never seems tired but is incessantly whipping them up to their utmost vigour. A steel rope, vibrating under strain, is perhaps an apt description of him. Most conductors who use great energy and vitality have strong physical frames: but where Sargent keeps that inexhaustible energy in his spare body is beyond comprehension.

Though he is so successful with the orchestra he achieves a still greater success with a choir—and the rougher it is, the better. To see him at work with a choir at a country festival is, perhaps, to see him in his most inspired moments. He is able to instil into the singers a life and efficiency they never dreamed of. You have only to see the eyes of a choral society screwing into him like hundreds of gimlets, to understand what he means to them. He is hypnotic with the choir—he plays upon the imagination and minds of the singers like a mesmerist. The Royal Choral Society is a wonderful instrument in his hands.

His fluency of speech reflects his quick mind. He is never at a loss for a word, the right one is always at the tip of his tongue. This particular gift serves him admirably at his concerts for children; there one sees Sargent completely at home. His understanding of the child-mind is perfect, and even hardened orchestral players enjoy seeing happy relations between him and his Saturday morning audience. Sargent has given his children such lessons as children have never had anywhere else in the world.

The orchestra is sometimes a scratch one, but there is nothing he likes better as long as the players are expert. He has a short rehearsal of major points and gives a few special instructions to those who have to show off their instruments.

"Brass, I want you to stand up as I call you out, one by one, and just play a few notes of a scale to show the children the sound and compass of your instruments."

Then, after a few minutes' interval, the orchestra assembles again and he introduces to the children the particular section of the orchestra with which he is dealing, whereupon the whole vast audience of the Westminster Central Hall becomes as quiet as in church. He holds them fast in his hand while in an effortless and brilliant little lecture he describes the orchestral instruments and gives a concise and imaginative explanation of the programme. Sargent has blessed this generation of children with something unknown to children of the past. His power lies in his ability to express himself in terms any child can understand. Then, after the talk, he does what few other conductors could achieve with so little time, giving a first-class performance of the programme. It is doubtful whether any one else could do the two things so admirably.

When rehearsing for a symphony concert he hardly stops talking, or, if not talking, he is singing his inexhaustible "Yăttātā-Yăttătātā-Yăttāttă." Only Ansermet has a finer vocabulary of rhythmical vocalization. Sargent uses every moment of his rehearsal time. He pulls up as much at his last rehearsal as at his first. He does not believe in leaving to the inspiration of the moment or to the experience and skill of the players anything that can be cut and dried first at the rehearsal.

The first movement of Haydn's 'Drum Roll' Symphony shows his method of rehearsing. He plays as far as the end of the introduction, and stops.

"Gentlemen, it is very good, but it must be still more cool and quiet, and I want a lovely colour. This difficult introduction gives the atmosphere to the whole work. Bassoons, I shan't mind if you have a little reed trouble and don't play. I can't have it quiet enough, and I know it is difficult for you. First violins, I want that *appoggiatura* played just as a little grace-note—not two equal quavers. It is a different feeling from the other, which I think is wrong. Now, gentlemen, let us begin again. Timpani, only a very *piano* roll. It is the next time you have it that I want more sound."

He stops again in the last three or four bars—

"Strings, you know you are all, or mostly all, making a *crescendo* on those G's after the *sforzandi*. I know it's probably an unconscious one, but you must be careful. You let your bows run away and I get more sound instead of a quiet, even *piano*."

When he comes to the *allegro*, an immense amount of detailed work is carried out, especially in the first section. He stops every few bars and repeats passages over and over again.

"No, gentlemen, I don't feel we have got this right at all. It is far too hectic. I want this movement played *grazioso* rather than *scherzando*. Now in the second bar, for instance, first violins, you snatch at your semiquavers. I want them strictly in time,—Tōm-pŏttŏttŏttăttūm-Tōm-pŏttŏttŏ-tă tūm."—(*ad. lib.*)

He repeats the first seven bars a few times and stops again at the eighth.

"No, gentlemen, there are many of you too soon on

those semiquavers. Hold that crotchet and put the slightest accent on the first semiquaver, so that it is clearly heard; and always in this first section play your quavers short." At the scale passage about fourteen bars further on, he emphasizes the same trouble of the *tutti* passage being too fast and blurred—

"Don't hurry it, gentlemen. I only want it absolutely in time—Pŏ-ddă-ddŏ-ddă-ddă-ddă-ddă-ddă-dōm! You start the passage too soon you know, and rush it too much."

The *fortissimo*, a few bars later, causes him to exclaim—

"Gentlemen, I do not get a *fortissimo* from you at all at this point. It is the first *fortissimo*, and I want everything you've got; you should come forward on your chairs and toes! I won't be satisfied with anything! I must have terrific force and energy."

The next point he touches upon is the figure which appears in the second subject of the *allegro*—quaver, two semiquavers, quaver—

"Now this figure, Tūm-pŏtt-ttă-tā, Tūm-pŏttătt-tā—I want it very short and crisp. The last quaver must be particularly short—you will see later on, before the double bar, where it comes in *forte*. There Mr. B—— suggests this bowing—Down-down-up-down, down-down-up-down, down-down-up-down. I think it is very good, as it ensures that short quaver that I want."

Having played the last few bars once or twice to clear up these points before he goes on, he says,

"Now, gentlemen, let's do the whole of this first section again with the repeat—one moment—in these last three bars give me strong, equal notes, each quaver strong and vigorous. All I hear is Dā-de-Dā-de-Dā, and the other quaver disappears."

In the next part of the movement he asks for a change of mood.

"Here, I want the quaver played longer, the whole mood more *dolce* and *legato*; there must be far more *diminuendo* in the second violins, which must be just a slight little rhythmical sound—and together, gentlemen. Second violins, play that by yourselves—no, some of you are not looking at me at all! Gentlemen, I must have your eyes the whole time. You know that passage by heart, so you need not glue your eyes on the music."

At the pause he directs 'cellos and violas to play the quavers very dark and gloomy in tone and *legatissimo*.

"You have the main tune of the symphony in a new form. And, firsts and seconds, your descending phrases—give me much more *diminuendo*. Don't end it with a bump; it must be a long sigh. Mr. B—— suggests tying the last crotchet on with the bow. Yes, I think that's a good idea; mark it, please, all of you."

Two bars before the next pause he warns the strings to take breath after the quaver rest.

"Gentlemen, here and at the pause you must play absolutely on the stick. I don't want a pause, but just the slightest breath before you play the quavers. Give me again six bars before the pause."

The rest of the movement he continues to rehearse in the same detailed manner, touching on one or two new points. He asks for tremendous power at the dramatic *fortissimo* chords with strong *tremolando*.

"The whole essence of this movement is *dramatic*, not lyrical. You must get this feeling into it the whole time. You know, gentlemen, I don't feel that you are keeping up your emotion; it sounds and looks flabby. I must have every ounce of vitality in you the whole time—and that figure—Tūm-pŏtt-ŏtt-tā, Tūm-pŏtt-ŏtt-tā—is not yet rhythmical and vital enough. You don't seem to take enough time; some of you are still playing the quavers too long. 'Cellos and violas, try your utmost to make this absolutely clear in the last bars of the movement."

At the performance Sargent's power of control is always completely reliable and efficient; there is never a moment of hesitation or nervousness. His eyes are always upon the players, never lost in the score, and each new tempo is set with unmistakable clarity. He is in command of every phrase and his soloists in the orchestra are directed rather than accompanied. Control and the joy of control show clearly in his face. It is inspiring to see him direct some great concert with a huge choir and enlarged orchestra. He invariably rises to the height of the great occasion, and with supreme confidence and enjoyment of mastery "puts a performance across" in a way few can surpass. Sargent is the personification of efficiency. Incredibly versatile, in every one of his activities he is masterly.

ARTURO TOSCANINI

ARTURO TOSCANINI

HOW rare is the artist of whom we can truly say, "He is supreme!" A carping minority almost always has qualifications and strictures to make.

In any orchestra accustomed to play under famous conductors there are players ready to criticize and make damaging comparisons. The spirits of Richter and Nikisch are called up in the last resort if the conductor under discussion cannot be belittled by comparison with a living colleague. But against Toscanini even those great names are powerless. Toscanini is the one living conductor whom every single member of the orchestra approves.

Under Toscanini orchestral playing becomes a different art. He stimulates his men, refreshes their minds; and music that has become stale is revived in all its pristine beauty. Rehearsals are looked forward to. There is never a moment of dullness—everything is far too concentrated and vital— nor is there any vain repetition. The time-factor disappears. Sheer physical fatigue takes the place of the clock, which is so often watched hopefully when work is dull.

After a stiff piece of detailed rehearsing Toscanini will say, "Non va male! Bitte da capo, from the beginning." Such a demand from a boring conductor might bring a groan from the orchestra, which would suspect that the repetition was merely to afford him personal pleasure, or even just to fill up time. But with Toscanini there is no wasting a moment. Rehearsals finish as soon as he feels there is no more to be done. He is never satisfied, but he seems to have an exact picture of the utmost any orchestra can achieve. His continual striving for perfection is felt to apply to himself rather than to spring from dissatisfaction with the orchestra. If he cannot please himself he does not allow the players to feel they are to blame.

Giving out an intense vitality himself, he expects no less in return, but he realizes when the players are fatigued and he does not drive them harder than himself. When a sign of flagging shows he immediately breaks off and suggests a cigarette. Almost dead-beat himself at the end of two grilling hours over the Pastoral Symphony, he said: "I am tired now, and I am sure you are, too. Let us rest."

There is no question of playing on for his own pleasure. On a successful morning he may finish long before the appointed time. He even may, if well ahead with his preparations, cancel the next rehearsal. If he does, by exception, want something repeated for his own sake, he makes no bones about it. After running through Berlioz's 'Queen Mab', he remarked with a winning smile: "Bene! You play it bene! But me, no. Bitte, da capo!"

Rather a difference from the young conductor who quacks for an hour over a ten-minute work and then blithely exclaims: "And now we will do it all again!"

Without any cut-and-dried scheme, Toscanini covers all the ground at preliminary rehearsals, and the final rehearsal —with so many conductors a violent race against time—he directs with calm and smooth organization, though electrical in vitality. Only once or twice when he was in London last summer did he use up his full time at a day's rehearsal.

His final full rehearsal of a symphony will rise to the same height as at the concert itself, with the same care and expenditure of vitality on the part both of himself and the orchestra. But never does the rehearsal surpass the concert, as it is apt to do with some famous conductors who drive too hard at the last rehearsal and drain life from the performance proper.

A peculiar characteristic of his genius is his profound unawareness of the audience. The presence or absence of listeners makes not the slightest difference to his performance. If anything, his gestures are slightly more clear and pronounced at the concert, but his essential attitude is always the same. There is nothing of the showman in his constitution. One might say that he is untouched by the audience, were it not that a man of such power must derive some deep psychological impetus from listeners so completely enthralled.

His modest, deprecatory gesture after the concert, sharing the honours with the orchestra, is utterly natural. Whatever the ovation, having appeared once or twice in an increasing tumult, he whispers to the principal first violin to lead the orchestra from the platform—and that's the end.

Concentration, the most intense concentration, is the direction which Toscanini's strength takes, in study as in performance. It may be that his affliction of acute shortsight has helped to give him that unselfconscious stance. We all know that closed eyes assist concentration and memory. This concentration of his, which must be very near the root of his greatness, enables him to live and think the music he is recreating so deeply and intensely that all who are working with him feel drawn to the composer's very heart. It is a state of mind which blots out everything save the subject desired; he enters into another world, taking the orchestra with him. It is frequently noticeable at rehearsal that when he is deeply engaged upon a line of thought and anything unexpectedly happens to snap it, he reacts violently, though at the performance proper nothing seems to upset him.

Once he has started, a slight mistake brings no calamitous look to his face. Yet at rehearsal, if he is building up a climax and a heavy instrument just fails to rise to the occasion by not giving its utmost power, Toscanini will become violent. Score and stick will fly and inferno is let loose for a moment or two.

I have it from an eye-witness that not long ago he was rehearsing the 'Eroica' symphony in a European capital. The first and second movements were played straight through, and the orchestra began to think that all was well. This was, however, the calm before the storm— which burst after the *scherzo*. Leaving the platform in a rage, Toscanini refused to return unless five or six changes were made in the personnel. Although all seats had been sold, the concert had to be postponed for five days and the orchestra reconstituted.

Possibly Toscanini has good reason for the occurrence from time to time of such incidents, which have their use in reinforcing his peremptory demand for respect and for the utmost that players can give him. So celebrated is his temper that it is the more pleasure to be able to say that his relations with the B.B.C. Orchestra have hitherto been invariably happy.

Intolerable to him are carelessness and anything like second-rateness and inefficiency. He seems to perceive it by instinct, if the players are giving their best. If not, he will break off and exclaim furiously: "I understand you make the mistake once, yes, but I do not understand you make it a second time. Santo Dio! Via, via, via! Take care!"

When upset he speaks more and more quickly, his voice thrilling with passion, and if he is extremely angry he breaks into voluble Italian, spiced with a variety of French and German. His English is quite adequate for normal needs. At times a word may fail him. Then there is a moment or two of intense thought and he suddenly comes out with an idiom, spoken without a trace of accent.

His explanations are sung in a conductor's unlovely voice which seems to be attempting double-stops, or else breaks into falsetto. Like Sir Thomas Beecham's, its compass is strictly limited, but it serves the purpose and the feeling it expresses is unmistakable. He does not care for long explanations. Almost everything is done with baton and gesture or by his singing.

The motif of every rehearsal is "Cantando, sempre cantando!" "You must sing every note you play, sing even through your rests!" "Not only play correctly; sing, molto cantando, all the time!" "Ah, cantare, cantare!" "Music, unless you sing, is nothing."

Along with Toscanini's gift of unique concentration goes

his unfailing servant—his prodigious memory. It must be understood that he really remembers everything to the minutest detail. There is no misty place in that mind, no doubtful background in that vision. He instantly detects a colour that is a shade incorrect. When focussing upon a certain passage at rehearsal he will sing bar after bar of the second clarinet's part or the fourth horn's, though it may have no melodic form whatever but only filling-up harmonies.

He must absolutely know every separate instrumental part of his scores from memory. This, indeed, he frequently proves, and never more than when dealing with secondary harmonies and chording. Instead of merely pointing to a false note or fault of balance, he will sing one part of a whole progression of chords, if he is concentrating on a particular instrument. He applies this focussing faculty very largely to accompanying figures and backgrounds, and, indeed, spends as much time on such things as on the curving of a lovely melody or the building of climaxes.

The care he took with the sustained harmonies of the lower strings accompanying the opening of the 'Enigma' Variations in the summer of 1935, when he first conducted an English orchestra, is still vividly remembered. This was actually at the beginning of his first rehearsal, and his words are recalled. "It is only 'armony, yes, but it is lovely music and it must be alive. For me it is too dead." Then he had a few bars played only on violas and 'cellos, several times, until it satisfied him and was as sensitive and coloured as the theme itself.

Toscanini is excessively short-sighted. To see him peering

at a score, held so that it nearly touches his nose, is to begin
to understand how his memory holds fast its multitude of
details. Evidently to read thus laboriously is in a measure
to memorize. It is sometimes painful to see him search for
a rehearsal letter in a score or for some other point that has
eluded him.

He rehearses everything from memory, merely referring
to the score for rehearsal numbers or for confirmation of a
detail, over which he is right 99 times in 100. His scores
seem almost unannotated; yet he never forgets a particular
thing he has asked for. He uses any score of the classics
which happens to be provided, only bringing his own for
unfamiliar works. Occasionally he brings his own orchestral
parts—not all very good, and some too bad to be used. None
meticulously marked as, for instance, are Mengelberg's.

The legend is unfounded which says that Toscanini never
notates a classic and never even slightly alters the original
markings; but the exceptions are exceptional enough to
belong to the sort that proves the rule. A typical modifica-
tion is his *pianissimo* at the beginning of the long *crescendo*
in the first movement of the Pastoral Symphony, instead
of Beethoven's *piano*; he thus adds to the greatness of the
climax he is aiming at.

In 'Coriolan' the exceptions to the rule are more considerable, particularly in the accompaniment to the second
subject, the strong relief with which he brings out the
quaver and crotchet. Then in the arpeggios for 'cellos and
violas he marks a great *crescendo* and *diminuendo* in each bar.
Near the end of this overture he introduces—a great rarity
with Toscanini—a change of tempo quite unindicated in the

score. Can it be denied that the result is superbly Beethovenian? 'Coriolan' was the only classic in which he made such considerable departures. The 'Eroica' was read as it was written, untouched.

In Brahms Toscanini may, when the balance is not satisfactory, adjust the strength of an important part, but he relies on the intelligence of the orchestra to read between the lines in those passages where the scoring is not very clear. In Haydn and Mozart he is fairly free with nuances, but the expression marks he adds are, after all, but slight ones, such as any good musician would apply to music left so bare by the composer. He is free, too, with his editing of Corelli, Cherubini and Rossini.

Toscanini is not a purist in a rigid sense, and when interpreting the early classics he does not hesitate to bring the utmost out of the music. Thus, in the rise and fall of a melody to which the composer has probably given no marks of expression he will make a natural *crescendo* and *diminuendo* or he may alter the colour in a repetition. But in Beethoven and his successors he more and more implicitly obeys the composer's directions. And, of course, in modern music— not in great masterpieces only, but also in all lesser works. And always his passionate desire is to represent with the utmost truthfulness the composer's mind.

All music seems alike to Toscanini in this respect, that everything he plays he plays as though it were his favourite and adored piece. Lavishing his heart and soul on second-rate compositions, he can make them seem great works of art. Always he brings to his scores a fresh mind, as though he has just come upon a fascinating discovery. He unmis-

takably loves playing some Italian music which, with the
best will in the world, one can only call second-rate. He
spent hours rehearsing Tommasini's 'Venetian Carnival',
and was like a boy with a toy as the orchestra exerted itself
to read appalling passages at sight and to make the work
sound like a masterpiece.

Toscanini's concentration is communicated to the
orchestra before he has said a word or lifted a finger.
He collects himself, and in so doing compels all to do
the same. In that frame of mind false starts, the bugbear of
many rehearsals, are impossible. He names the piece to be
played; and there, as for a few moments he stands still, he
seems to be presented with the whole picture of the work in
his mind's eye.

There are two unique characteristics of his not otherwise
very extraordinary stick. First is the magnificent sweep,
which must be one of the most eloquent gestures ever made
and which seems to hold all the threads of the orchestra and
to imbue them with life. Secondly, there is his not so apparent, but extraordinarily dynamic, almost magical preparation for his beats. The former holds audience and orchestra
alike; in the latter only the orchestra can appreciate the
wonderful anticipation of the beat. The most difficult
change of tempo becomes, even to those farthest from him,
clear and unmistakable just at the right moment. This
lightning anticipation in his up-beats is never more effective
than in passages where the percussion is, generally because
of distance, apt to lag. It suddenly finds itself whipped up,
and the whole orchestra shot with a terrific rhythmic
impulse.

M

Toscanini holds his stick stiffly, never using wrist or fingers independently. The first finger is always rigidly extended along the baton, rather like Weingartner's. It does not by any means always come to rest at a given point; yet in chording and difficult ensemble no player seems to doubt where it will stop. Even to those on the fringe of the orchestra this is quite clear. Only one doubt seems to occur: Toscanini sometimes does not give a clear indication of the finish of a chord, and one may hear a little raggedness in held notes.

Personal magnetism achieves everything else for him. It radiates from the man and holds each of us, not in a grip of iron, but with a power at once irresistible and intensely human and sympathetic. Toscanini is aloof, he makes no contacts with the players, except perhaps the leader; one wonders whether he recognizes any of them by face, though he certainly does by their playing. But he is no superman; he is a truly human being.

His body is very flexible and turns freely. The second violins get as much help as the firsts. His body seems always to be facing the chief interest. At the beginning of the storm in the Pastoral Symphony he turns full to the seconds, then right round to the firsts on their entry; yet his stance appears very stable and he makes scarcely a movement with his feet.

The rehearsals are a great strain on the orchestra. Toscanini's concentration is apt to make him overwrought. A player, engaged on a long solo, may be giving forth his utmost skill and artistry; yet something in the style or colour may conflict with the vivid picture in Toscanini's mind, and he will suddenly stop, slam his desk with his stick, and exclaim in a furious voice: "Why don't you look at me? There is no stringendo there; why do you make one? Andiamo, andiamo! Sing the music! It is so beautiful, and you play cold! Andiamo! Da capo, oboe and flute."

A flash of passion is liable to burst out at almost any time. Yet Toscanini also possesses a wonderful patience, especially in some episode he knows to be unusually difficult for the orchestra as a whole or for a particular department. He had hard work to get a perfect ensemble between the solo viola and oboe in the first movement of Debussy's 'Iberia'. After two or three attempts, imperfect intonation and ensemble between the two instruments were almost more than he could bear, so he suggested that the viola should move up to sit next the oboe. This made for a better result, but after two or three more attempts there was still something to be desired. His face expressed exquisite pain, but with a charming smile—"Never mind, da capo again! Patience, we must have patience. It is terribly difficile." At last it became clear and was not touched again at any rehearsal.

He had some trouble in the closing bars of Wagner's 'Forest Murmurs'. The first violins were not clear in their ascending arpeggio, so he tried them by themselves three or four times, and at length it came right. He did not rehearse it again at all. At the concert it was perfect.

It has been remarked sometimes that he passes over fluffy passages as it were in spite of himself. This is true; but it is unlikely that it will be allowed twice. Generally such things occur in episodes of no great importance, when he has got into his stride and the piece is going well. On the other hand, a slip may happen in a department upon which his searchlight is turned, and with a sudden slash of his stick on the desk—"Andiamo! Andiamo! What a pity! It was going bene; why did you spoil it? Ah, what a pity, what a pity!" (Turning to his score)—"Now, where is it? Via! via! via! You must take care!" Then it may take him many precious and painful moments to find the place in the score.

The orchestra never knows when this delicately poised balance of his may be upset, and consequently is always on tenterhooks; yet the nervousness he induces is essentially helpful for playing—not paralysing. Every player in the orchestra knows that he stops or repeats a passage only for a vital reason. There are conductors who frequently stop to air their knowledge, and also possibly to try to "find out" the orchestra. Toscanini never plays the schoolmaster or lectures the orchestra. No conductor, save Weingartner perhaps, talks less. Toscanini never says a word about himself or his work.

Almost every conductor is known to the orchestra by some little mannerism or catchword. It may be a special rhythmical idea, or certain sentences he employs to obtain an effect. Thus, Bruno Walter's "Più piano!"; Mengelberg's "Ter-Der!"; Albert Coates's "Extase colour!"; Sir Henry Wood's inimitable "Play near the bridge! Let your tone penetrate!" Toscanini's unceasing cry, "Singing, cantando, ah, cantando sempre! Always cantare!" echoes long after the others. This one word "cantando" expresses all that he desires so intensely from his orchestra.

The most anxious time for the orchestra comes at the opening of a movement, especially at the very beginning of a symphony. The opening of the 'Pastoral' was played again and again until the mood, phrasing, and in particular the long *crescendi* became perfectly balanced. So it was with 'Coriolan', and Brahms's C Minor, and in fact all the major works. The 'Eroica' was the exception. The first movement and the scherzo were almost untouched. The second and last movements were rehearsed in detail. The very end of the slow movement was taken with the greatest care of all. The wailing cry of the first violins did not satisfy him for a long time. Finally the wonderful ending of this movement seemed almost unbearable in its sorrow, even at rehearsal. Again and again he worked at this, saying not a word save for "Like a cry!" but each time getting a little nearer his vision. Occasionally he seeks help by suggesting a picture to the orchestra to describe something. In 1935 he actually told us always to have a picture in our minds of the music we were to play. He will sometimes suggest an emotion, as in the Preislied section of the overture to 'Meistersinger'. "First violins, play *sotto voce*, but with intense feeling, as if you said" (whispering to himself) "'I love you, I love you!'—but whispered, under your breath!" An expression like this will frequently come out spontaneously, especially after he has been at a loss for the right English word.

When he is baffled by the lack of a word, or possibly some elusive point in the score, he reflects deeply and after a moment or so generally finds it. His memory is like the slave of Aladdin's lamp—it always appears, faithfully obedient to his wish. As for the score itself, his grasp of it is practically perfect. Only once during the 1937 festival did he refer to the score and find his memory at fault. At one place in the 'Siegfried Idyll', near the beginning, where the violas have a dotted minim at the end of a phrase, he expressed surprise that they were holding it so long, and referring to the score he noted that they were right. That forgotten dot was the solitary mistake his memory made.

When he begins his rehearsals for such a festival he asks for no rearrangement of the orchestra seating, but just looks round, asks for the principal player in each department to make sure of his position, and immediately begins work. He does not play straight through a movement to feel the orchestra and accustom himself to the hall, but either stops the moment he has anything to say, or else saves his comments until the end. Within three minutes the orchestra might have been rehearsing with him for days.

Some conductors, after being introduced to the orchestra, observe the seating, and forthwith mutter "Impossible!" Then there has to be a general post to alter the whole placing of the players. This may take an hour. Toscanini altered nothing.

There is a certain atmosphere at a rehearsal with Toscanini which is unique, and it is apparent before his arrival on the platform, not only for the first rehearsal but for every one. He will never come to the platform unless there is complete silence, with tuning already adjusted throughout the orchestra. As a mark of particular respect the players all stand for him each morning; this is always greeted by a smiling "Good morning!" An orchestra may completely upset him by the usual tuning which greets many conductors. The beginnings of all parts of his work are vitally important for this extraordinary atmosphere of intensity, which never relaxes while he is on the rostrum. Tuning he will not tolerate, unless he personally orders it; if adjustments are vital they must be made without his hearing a sound. And he has acute hearing. Unlike Mengelberg, he takes no part himself in this matter. It simply has to be correct; and woe betide the offenders!

He is always in the artists' room at least fifteen minutes before rehearsal, and extraneous noises before a rehearsal, when he is already concentrating on a score, are unbearable to him. He is always dressed in a black alpaca coat, buttoned military fashion up to the throat, with striped trousers. For the first part of the rehearsal he wears a stiff white collar and cuffs, but after the interval he has become so hot that these are discarded.

After an appreciative gesture and a pleased smile in answer to the orchestra's tribute each morning, he quietly and quickly mounts the rostrum, and searches for the score he wants. He frequently begins work by turning to a minor point, searching painfully in his short-sighted way for a reference-letter, and getting impatient if he cannot find it. Then he may direct, say, the 3rd clarinet, six bars after Letter B, where he is playing a semibreve G, to play with a *crescendo* for half the bar and *diminuendo* for the second half, and not as it is printed—a continued *diminuendo*. And to emphasize this he makes the actual sign with two fingers of each hand: < > . Details such as this frequently open the rehearsal before a note is played. Toscanini always gives the impression that his mind has been busy with the score long before he arrives on the platform.

While the orchestra prepares to play, he always reflects deeply for a moment or two, in a characteristic attitude—head slightly bent down, the baton held upright close to his body, its tip just touching his chin. Then, with his preparatory words in three languages—"Bien—bitte—allora !" he taps his desk sharply with the baton and immediately plays as far as possible, not stopping for minor details, but saving them up in his head for either an enforced stop or the end of the exposition of the movement. Most of the incorrect minor details are reflected by his expression, or by a click of his tongue. If all goes well, to his thinking, he does not play it again—he repeats nothing that is not absolutely necessary.

In London in 1937 he opened his rehearsals with Brahms's C minor symphony. He played it as far as the first double bar (after Fig. E) and then stopped. "Ah, non si male—some things, yes! First and second violins, speak clear your semiquavers, I do not hear them! Bitte, play first and second violins only, six bars after A! Speak clear and in tempo. Alors, bassoon, and first violin, also flute." (He sings the phrase six bars after Letter A.) "This beautiful music! Ah, why do you not sing? Sempre cantare, sempre cantare, always, always sing! Alors—da capo, the beginning."

After one or two more stops one realizes the unusual tautness of the atmosphere. There is dead silence at a stop, with no stragglers or hushed whispers. Frequently at a rehearsal the conductor stops, and a straggler or two goes on playing. With Toscanini, silence is instantaneous and may almost be felt.

Before beginning the Andante he asks the orchestra to "Play *piano*, espressivo, in tempo and cantando!" After a few bars he stops, and reminds the lower strings of the pianissimo at the third bar. Once again he plays the opening, and proceeds as far as the entry of the oboe, when he again stops after two or three bars of the solo. "Ah, cantando! It is so cold—it is impossible to play unless you sing." He sings these last bars of the oboe solo with the most intense feeling, his voice breaking into falsetto as he overloads it with emotion. Impossible not to be dominated by that amazing, pent-up emotion which at times seems to burst from him. If he receives a good response, then he is happy; but if for some reason this is lacking he seems to feel a sickening sense of frustration; he drives himself almost frantic in endeavouring to express the vision that is so clear to him but cloudy to the orchestra.

"Oh, why cannot you see? I do this or that—look at me! It is impossible not to understand. Ah, andiamo! andiamo! I do not make stringendo or ritenuto. In tempo, play in tempo, and sing. I do not ask more, but cantare with me." All these disjointed phrases pour from his mouth, and he stamps on his rostrum in a frenzy, loose pages flying from his score.

A bar or two farther on the lower strings crowd in too soon on the first violin *sforzando*, and Toscanini warns them that it is a full quaver later. At the oboe solo, Letter B (second subject), he seizes on the accompaniment in the lower strings. "Not sec, but smooth and alive!—a slight push on the first note! Oboe, you play correct, yes, you play too correct; you must put something inside. Cantando, sempre cantando!"

Nineteen bars before C he stops again, and remarks: "This is the only place in the movement where it is poco agitato." The four-times-repeated figure, commencing on the flute and ending with the first violin, he directs in one long *diminuendo*, and plays the passage once or twice to get a perfect join between each of the phrases; and then continues to the end. After an encouraging "Bene!" he warns the orchestra always to be ready in resuming the tempo in this movement. "It is difficile, but in this movement if we make little rallentandi we must at once resume the tempo."

The third movement is taken very light and feathery. A sign of irritation shows in Toscanini's face as rather heavy weather is made between 'cellos and basses on the one hand and the upper strings on the other, at Letter B (in the reiterated semiquavers). This passage introduced his first exclamations of "Take care! Via! via! via! It is not clear; 'celli, you are late, and basses too—play by yourselves. In tempo, in tempo. No stringendo or rallentando, absolument in tempo."

When dealing with some difficult ensemble like this, or any technical difficulties, he immediately asks for the instruments concerned only. Having achieved perfection once, he does not ask for it again. The last movement he rehearsed very little, building the whole movement up to a terrific height at the *più allegro*, and capping it with the chorale played in exactly the same *tempo*, thus breaking with the usual tradition of *molto largamente*.

Throughout the festival no work was over-rehearsed, and a few, like the last movement of the Brahms, were just played through once. The first movement and the scherzo of the 'Eroica' were played through once only at a preliminary rehearsal, and then only a few bars of each touched again. On the other hand, the Funeral March was closely rehearsed, particularly the closing bars and the building up of the fugue; as also was the whole of the last movement. At the final rehearsal of the finale he spent a great deal of time upon clear ensemble in the opening variations, and also in the perfect "taking over" from instrument to instrument over the double bars and repeats.

This detailed work at a final rehearsal is unusual for him and there was a terrific explosion when the playing of the *poco andante* suddenly aroused his ire. Up to that point it was going exceedingly well, when without any warning he seized the open score as if it were going to be torn to bits, loose pages flying out, and stamped round the rostrum, a torrent of Italian streaming from his lips, appealing to all the saints and to the Deity himself. "Why do you change the tempo? You make stringendo and rallentando—why, why, why?" And then another stream of Italian, mixed with French and German. His face, of rare beauty in repose, becomes almost terrifying in fury. However, a storm such as this lasts but a little while and does not colour the rest of the rehearsal in the least. This particular passage was played once or twice, for the balance did not satisfy him, but it was almost the only occasion of a serious explosion.

In no great music does he seek to impose his mind on that of the composer, but is always and tirelessly trying to interpret with the utmost truth. It is seldom that he is frustrated in this; but when for some reason he cannot "speak clear" to the orchestra, to use his own words, then the apple-cart will be upset. It is amazing that he is able so easily to translate that superb vision in his mind, just by means of quiet gesture. For pages and pages of a score he seems in complete accord, and having once become sure of a perfect response he never changes a tempo or an expression mark, so that the orchestra is never anxious at a concert. Yet his performance always seems spontaneous. If he has asked for any detail he never forgets. "But I do not understand—I told you that note must have special accent, two days ago. I do not forget. Via! via! via! Take care!"

In lesser works he allows his creative power more scope —not arbitrarily but by making them sound like master-pieces. Though his performance of a Beethoven symphony may be great, he will make a piece like Strauss's 'Tod und Verklärung' stand up to it by the sheer beauty of his conviction. In this piece his intensity of rehearsal was especially marked. He rehearsed closely the whole of the introduction, for the sake of tranquillity and perfect intona-tion. Endless pains were taken at the very opening, over the little rhythmic pulsing figure, and then over the intona-tion of the wood-wind solos. "Ah, this introdooshun—it is so difficile! Always I have trouble; we must have patience!" "Third trombone and cor anglais—it is so out of tune! Take care! Trombone, I think you are a little sharp. Cor anglais, you must listen and help a little. Try and tune" (with an expression of acute discomfort on his face)—"it is still bad." "Third trombone, you are now a little flat. But the C bemolle, it is too high." "Now, harp and flute, please, together. Ah, I want it so calm—it is so beautiful!"

The rest of the work was rehearsed just as carefully, including the whole middle 'Fever' section, with terrific emotion and fire. A dreadful explosion took place at the end of this section, at the *ff* after the *sforzando* on the violas —opened by the bass tuba *ff*. For some reason it did not tell sufficiently. Toscanini went livid. "Why, bass tuba, do you play like muted violin? It is *fortissimo*."

And then streams of words in three or four languages, and the back of the score dreadfully wrenched and baton hurled on the floor. The violas, sitting round him with frightened, upturned faces, wondered what was coming next. Yet after a terrible outburst he calmed down to utter tranquillity after the moment of "dissolution," which was amazingly impressive by its complete adherence to the score and strict observance of *diminuendo*, with practically no *ritenuto*. The climax at the end of the work was something that had to be heard to be believed. Piled up and up with ever something in reserve, until the great moment of all, which was shatter- ing. Right through this work of Strauss—as in all the Wagner pieces, too—not the slightest alteration was made in the score; yet the work sounded quite fresh, and much of it as though unheard before. And this Strauss piece is generally considered very stale by the orchestra.

All technical difficulties and passage work seem to become more playable with Toscanini. He feels the tempo at which a piece will sound must effective. In works like Elgar's 'Introduction and Allegro' the playing depends on correct tempo to ensure the utmost clarity and brilliance. Toscanini's genius lies in his being always able to reconcile this fact with the composer's own directions. It is a very subtle matter, and perhaps not perceived at all by the audience, but the orchestra is supremely conscious of it. Only a hair's breadth lies between ease and great difficulty in a technical matter, and Toscanini succeeds invariably in finding ease.

We in the orchestra are on closer terms with the conductor than any one else, and are in an unassailable position to judge whether he is making music from his heart or from his head. Let it be well and truly understood that in Toscanini the two are in perfect balance. All his music-making springs from his inmost being, though his mind directs his heart, as every member of the orchestra is made aware in the first five minutes of his rehearsal. He is completely caught up in the music, and every line of his face shows the depth and intensity of his feeling. And it pours from him. The fact that he is master of this power does not mean that he is dishonest with himself, but that all power on earth, to be effective, has to be in control. Look at him in the act of building up a climax. He asks more and more, until the orchestra's breath and strength are almost used up, and then from his reserves he gives forth still more of himself, until the most vital point of all is reached. He never allows his forces to expend themselves to waste, nor does he ever over-paint a phrase.

His crowning glory is the presentation of a work with such divine simplicity that it suddenly appears in a new and fresh light—yet, incredibly, only as the composer left it.

SIR HENRY WOOD

SIR HENRY WOOD

SIR HENRY WOOD celebrates this year—1938—his jubilee as a conductor. His record is impressive, and is indeed not to be paralleled. To think of the cavalcade of composers and of executive artists who have passed before him in those fifty years of concerts is to feel almost dizzy, and many from both ranks owe their success to his early recognition. He has at the same time trained the majority of orchestral players himself. Comparatively few who are now in the best orchestras have not at some time or other passed through his hands, either in the old Queen's Hall orchestra, at the Promenade concerts or at the Royal Academy of Music. He may be called, in truth, the father of our orchestras.

To consider for a moment the Queen's Hall Promenade concerts alone—and they have represented only a fraction of his activities—it is not conceivable that anyone else, living now or in the past, could have called upon the physical and mental powers necessary to stay such a course. One season is a formidable strain, let alone forty or more of them. No other conductor in the world possesses such a repertory. All his famous colleagues set some bounds to their activities, but Sir Henry is infinite. Remember, too, that in the hundreds and thousands of works he has studied, there are masses that he has had to relegate to limbo, never to be played again. It is amazing that the litter has never swamped his mind. One or two of his early Promenade programmes are given here to show the way he has cleared for the present taste:

PROMENADE CONCERT
TUESDAY, AUG. 13TH, 1895

Overture—'Le Domino Noir' – – –	*Auber*
Song—'Ailsa Mire' – – – – –	*Newton*
(*a*) Intermezzo for Strings – – –	*Allan Macbeth*
(*b*) Bohemian Dance—'La Jolie Fille de Perth'	*Bizet*
Aria—'Sognai' – – – – – –	*Schira*
Scène du Bal—'Le Roi S'Amuse' – –	*Delibes*
Recit. and Air—'O Ruddier than the Cherry'	*Handel*
(*a*) Nocturne in E flat ⎱ orchestrated by Müller-	
(*b*) Polonaise in A ⎰ Beighaus – –	*Chopin*

INTERVAL OF FIFTEEN MINUTES

Grand Selection—'The Gondoliers' – –	*Sullivan*
Song—'Good Bye' – – – – –	*Tosti*
Solo Cornet—'Love's Old Sweet Song' –	*Molloy*
Song—'The Promise of Life' – – –	*Cowen*
Gavotte—'Regrets, Espérance' – –	*Michiels*
Song—'The Templar's Soliloquy' – – –	*Sullivan*
March—'Les Enfants de la Garde' – –	*Schloesser*

PROMENADE CONCERT
FRIDAY, SEPT. 6TH, 1895
Military Night

Military March—orchestrated by Harold Vicars	*Schubert*
Overture—'Les Dragons de Villars' –	*Meillant*
Aria—'Valse Song' (Romeo and Juliet) – –	*Gounod*

The German Patrol	–	–	–	–	– *Elenbery*
Recit. and Air.—'Sound an Alarm'			–	–	*Handel*
Military Overture in C	–	–	–		*Mendelssohn*
Song—'The Soldier's Tear'	–	–	–	–	*Alex Lee*
Recitation—'The Defence of Lucknow'				–	*Tennyson*
Selection—'The Red Hussar'		–	–	–	

INTERVAL OF FIFTEEN MINUTES

The British Army Quadrilles		–	–	–	*Julien*
Song—'The Castilian Maid'		–	–	*Lisa Lehmann*
Cornet Solo—'Sweet Sixteen'		–	–	–	
Song—'The Temple of Light'		–	–	*J. Valentine Hall*
Drum Polka	–	–	–	–	– *Julien*
Song—'Jeannette and Jeannot'			–	– *Chas. W. Glover*
The Soldiers' Chorus—'Faust'		–	–	–	*Gounod*

To-day he conducts a tricky new work, like a Bartók concerto, with as much confidence and efficiency as he originally showed in a Sullivan overture. His maxim throughout his career has been to be well ahead of his audiences in taste, though taking care not to push on so far as to lose them. Invaluable was the companion he had in the early days of his enterprise at Queen's Hall—Robert Newman who ran the business side. It was a great partnership, Wood and Newman, and London was lucky in that they had such a wonderfully long innings.

When Wood began the Promenade concerts at Queen's Hall he had not a highly-trained orchestra of picked musicians. The training he had to do himself, with but three rehearsals a week, and no preliminary study with the orchestra. All this meant the acquirement of a fool-proof baton and the most clear-minded method of using every precious minute of his rehearsals. Instead of concentrating on a workable number of scores, he had to learn how to deal efficiently with everything in existence. This is the answer to the question—Why does he never conduct from memory? His mind would have been so littered with the refuse of bygone music that he could not have kept up with the requirements of the modern composer. Consequently in no circumstances whatever does he conduct from memory.

It is nothing short of marvellous that a man of his years, after all the strain to which he has submitted that devoted frame of his, can still realize the latest of contemporary works as clearly as any one. He might reasonably be expected to say, "No, I am too tired for that kind of thing now—leave it to the younger men!" Yet a day or two before these lines were written he was astonishing in the accompaniment to Ravel's piano concerto—a brute of a thing to conduct—after only rehearsal enough to play through the work once, and perhaps five minutes to spare. At night he conducted the concerto perfectly, with the orchestra relying securely upon his slightest gesture when a moment's hesitation on his part would have spelt disaster.

Wood has introduced far and away more new music to the British public than any one else. What he may feel personally about a new work he is conducting seldom appears to the orchestra. If the music is very violent and unpleasant he may confide the heart's bitterness to one or two of the leaders but rarely to the whole orchestra. He takes as much trouble with a work that is unintelligible and irritating as over a masterpiece.

"Why don't you look at my stick? It's clear enough! Every morning I practise my baton for half an hour in front of the glass!" This is one of his favourite sayings, and it is characteristic. His life seems to hinge on the clock.

His baton is without an equal. It affords a flawless example of a conductor's technique. His half-hour's practice in the morning has had the result that it is now as natural to him to use his baton as his voice. Before the B.B.C. took over the Promenade concerts, Wood's concerts had to be given with very scanty rehearsal. His first care, then, was to be unmistakably clear with his baton. In this he succeeded so completely that the remark used to be passed to all new and nervous members of his orchestra: "Don't worry! You may be reading at sight in public, but you can't possibly go wrong with *that* stick in front of you!"

"That stick" is as capable of a finished piece of work as the bow in the hands of an expert violinist. It always moves to a given point, and is never at any time vague or indeterminate. It is foolproof as far as the orchestra is concerned. Utterly different from Weingartner's stiff poise, it is free and held loosely at the finger-tips, and is adequate of itself to direct all time and nuance, without the help of the left hand. Wood's batons are precious. They are always painted white—and re-painted. They are fitted with a long, tapering cork handle and balanced like a bow. If he breaks one on the lid of the opened piano—a frequent trap—he mutters: "There you are, another ten-and-six gone! M, ge—st me another baton!"

As the audience must be aware, everything with Sir Henry is arranged and provided for. There is always a spare stick, pushed through a ring in his score-cage beside him, which immediately comes into action when its predecessor has met with an accident. Never in history has he broken his second stick, and he will never dispense with it in any circumstances. His stick has become a component part of his right hand; it is as flexible as a finger, and the tip becomes the focal point of the entire orchestra.

With some conductors the elbow has to be observed—the stick is merely delusive. And there are famous conductors who use their batons stiffly and awkwardly, obtaining their results from personality and magnetism. But Sir Henry, for all purposes of ensemble, relies completely upon the extreme tip of his baton. One of his secrets for clarity and attack lies in the preparation of his beat and in the vital importance he attaches to "breath-taking"—not in the wind only but also in the strings.

"Breathe together before the attack! Watch my stick —it shows you when to take breath for the chord." He loves giving object lessons with his baton to emphasize points like this, and perpetually demands that the orchestra "look at the stick". "You play without a conductor! The two sides of the orchestra are not together at all! You may think you are, but I know better. Every eye on the stick! There's a time-lag of one-fifth of a second per fifty feet— allow for it! And you, furthest away from me, must remember particularly and play dead on the tip of my baton. Don't play by y'ear!"

Wood's left hand is not exceptionally expressive. Mostly it emphasizes the work of his stick and gives the leads for the entries of all instruments. Few conductors are more helpful in this respect. In the days of the less experienced orchestra he nursed every entry it was possible for him to give, and if at rehearsal an instrument missed one entry Sir Henry would make quite sure that he did not miss it at the concert. In this respect he looks after all the soloists when accompanying a concerto or aria. Always his eye is upon them with their cue.

His stick is not just a time-beater, but with its big sweep or tiny movement it controls the dynamics as well. It is extremely flexible and, at the sudden division into sub-divided beats, a model of clarity. Never is there any doubt, in a long spread-out bar, where each beat lies. There is a Manchester story of this famous stick and its swish when moving with great speed. Wood was directing Mendelssohn's 'Wedding March' without a rehearsal at a popular concert. If he is not sure of his players he takes great care of the beginning and the entries, and frequently starts with an anticipatory beat to show a clear tempo. The trumpet on this occasion had evidently not been warned, or else through fright he misunderstood. For the opening trumpet fanfare on the fourth beat Sir Henry's stick described the three artificial beats—swish, swish, swish! But then nothing happened. Again,—"swish, swish, swish," accompanied by the click of his sleeve-links, rang out in the hall. And still silence. Eventually, history relates, he signed to the trumpet to start when he liked.

These were in early days. He is insistent now that one or two beats for nothing are amateurish. But for the sake of absolute precision at the beginning of a movement, starting at the last beat of the bar, he may still occasionally give an introductory beat, and to the orchestra it is far easier, especially in a case like the opening of the last movement of Schubert's C major symphony. At such times, at the opening of a piece in quick tempo or an off-beat, he considers the sacrifice of professionalism necessary for perfect ensemble.

Sir Henry's voice would, if he wished, penetrate a factory in full blast. It has tremendous power, and he knows precisely how to pitch it. If he is listening to a rehearsal at the back of a hall and wants to say something in the middle of a full *fortissimo*, his voice will reach every member of the orchestra. The great importance he attaches to "breathing" is due to his experience as a singing teacher, as many soloists have found out when singing arias at Promenade rehearsals. He never hesitates to criticize their breathing or a vocal point that displeases him. Once at a monster performance at the old Crystal Palace, rehearsing Verdi's 'Requiem', he came out with a most unusual remark to do with the art of breathing. One must have taken part in one of those undertakings to realize the vast numbers that used to be employed in the orchestra and chorus. In this case he also had two brass bands in the galleries at the far end of the transept. To aid the rehearsal he used a large dinner bell to bring things to a stop and a megaphone. His baton was freshly painted, and there was an electric push-button on the rostrum to warn the organ. The chorus was late with one or two entries, and through the megaphone Wood suddenly boomed: "You're late because you *will* breathe through your noses!—I don't want any nose-breathers here! Suck in air through your mouths!"

The orchestral players at times find themselves embarrassed when a well-known singer is hauled over the coals before them. ("What are you doing? But, my dear lady, you are not holding your quaver, so your rhythm goes to pieces. I know what it is, you want to bottle me up, and I won't *be* bottled up.") But they enjoy themselves in full measure when the soloist, having protracted the rehearsal by insufficient knowledge of the piece, provokes a devastating lecture on "Knowing your job". This is some slight compensation to the orchestra for the extra work involved.

There can never have been an occasion for lecturing Sir Henry for not knowing his job. And his job entails many things beside mere conducting and mastery of the scores. Outside the orchestra, few know the almost incredible amount of time he spends on the editing and correction of the orchestral parts—a job which most conductors, and even composers, would consider donkey-work. Until a year or two ago he performed no new work without first correcting and checking each individual part. Having checked it, he signs it at the top—"Corrected, Henry J. Wood."

An indefatigable worker, he gives ceaseless care to the most minute details. Having had bitter experience of wasting hours of rehearsal time through bad parts, he takes nothing for granted. He himself bows all the string parts before they ever come to the rehearsal. Nothing that can be prepared before the rehearsal is omitted, and his scores are all noted with the various beats he intends to take at each tempo. He will possibly change some of these as he rehearses, but nevertheless it is all worked out in his mind and recorded in blue pencil.

His rehearsals—especially in those days of only three rehearsals a week during the Promenade season—were all worked out to the minute, so much time being spent on each piece. (Sometimes, the orchestra thinks, whether this needs it or not.) In undertaking something like 700 or 800 pieces—no less constitutes the Promenade programmes—a normal conductor would be submerged, but Sir Henry is equipped to cope with it all. In fourteen years only two or three pieces have had to be replaced through something going wrong with rehearsal timing.

Only with that part of the allowance that falls to a composer does he become sometimes powerless, for he is generous towards composer-conductors, frequently letting them enjoy themselves to the upsetting of his plans. On returning to the rostrum, after a composer's session, he sadly scratches out two or three pieces with his blue pencil and launches on a tirade. "All these composers are the same! They all want extra time!—I don't know how I'm going to get through. One hour to rehearse 95 minutes' music and two arias! It doesn't matter, of course, *my* part of the concert!" Yet he somehow gets through.

The orchestra finds it strange that, with all his technique and personal knowledge of his players, he will often, when pressed for time, play through works that are extremely familiar, and leave dangerous ones, like live bombs, to blow up at one miscue. But such is his nerve and skill that catastrophes are of the utmost rarity. With much to be rehearsed there is not time for a moment's relaxation between the pieces. As one comes to an end he announces the next, and he is away again before the horns can empty their instruments. Working at this terrific pressure, he yet loses his temper extraordinarily rarely, even when tried to the limits of human endurance. He was once forced to leave Strauss's 'Don Quixote' untouched until the day of the concert. The work is recognized as one of the most difficult in the repertory. At the beginning of the rehearsal he discovered that his special arrangement of seating for this work had gone wrong—a rare misunderstanding, for it is one of his incessant cares that a rearrangement of seating is set in order well before rehearsal. However, on this occasion ten minutes or so were lost. A temperamental conductor would have torn out handfuls of hair. Instead of becoming overwrought Wood exclaimed indignantly: "I can't understand it! For twenty-two years I have always had my tuba sitting next to the bass clarinet for 'Don Quixote'. How can you get any ensemble if they are fifty feet apart? Gentlemen, do what you can for me and change places quickly." (Not so easy and quick, for three departments have to re-arrange themselves.) "I've already lost six and a half minutes; I can't understand it at all! We have done this work year after year."

After the loss of this valuable time he settles down quickly, only to find, after one or two stops, that the tuba has never played the work before.

"What! But we are playing this to-night! You can't *read* a work like this! Why can't I have the usual player?" Someone at the back murmurs that he is dead. "More time lost—I can't waste time over it now, you must do what you can!"

Fortunately the player is brilliant and gives him no

further anxiety. However, that is not the end. The last straw is a pathetic, thin squeak from the wind machine; another exclamation:

"Where's my wind machine? F.—, why didn't you fetch it from the Academy?"

Mr. F.—, very deferentially:—"I'm sorry, Sir Henry, we found it was broken." "What do you mean, broken?" "The framework has collapsed, sir." "But I had this specially stoutly made for me! Can't understand why it is broken! It was strong enough, and I bought the black satin myself from Marshall & Snelgrove at four and nine a yard! Let me hear what you can do with that thing you've got there."

A few more squeaks from the machine.

"But that's no use! Can't hear it at all! What have you got round it?" "Canvas, Sir Henry." "No use at all—must have satin. There's no swish about that. Strauss directs here in his score a wonderful sound, and that's nothing like it. Can't you turn the handle harder? That's a little better, but it's no good—piffling little sound!"

In spite of such mishaps and the irritation they must cause, he never loses his temper, and with a twinkle in his eye goes on with the huge task of bringing clarity and order out of the complications of the score. When really pressed for time and his singers are due to rehearse their aria at 12.41, Sir Henry will at 12.39 exclaim with penetrating voice, whilst still playing: "M—s, get the singers ready!" And precisely at 12.41 they will be pushed on the platform, with the last chord still echoing round the hall, and the stick upheld for the aria.

The conducting of arias is a particular feature of Wood's art. As a young man he went up and down the country conducting opera companies, and he knows the repertory of opera arias as well as the singers themselves, and all the various traps for the orchestra which occur in recitative, to say nothing of those awkward moments when singers give full vent to their emotion. All his beats are worked out and explained to the orchestra in detail. War is declared on those publishing firms who supply bad parts for arias. Carefully though his plans may be laid for the accompaniment of these arias, they may be upset by parts that are a mass of inaccuracy and illegibility. He has largely overcome the deficiency by buying a complete set of parts as well as the score immediately he undertakes to perform a work, so that his labour of editing and correcting has to take place only once. His library must be almost unique—it contains nearly everything he has ever played.

It is instructive to see a new work on the desk, particularly of a violent order by Hindemith, say, or Béla Bartók, with the printer's ink scarcely dry, and at the top of it, "Henry J. Wood—Corrected", in his own writing. On examining the part one finds that naturals and flats and other trifles are scratched out or inserted, all in his own handwriting, with countless directions for "In 6", "In 4", "Beat here" (after a cadenza), "Utmost ferocity", and so on. Such is his passion for laying out everything in apple-pie order before coming to rehearsal. Wood does not make great use of his memory, but writes everything down in the score. At a change of tempo, a big "In 6" or "In 3" will be scored in blue pencil across the page. Many other reminders or remarks are noted, such as "Near the bridge"—"Bad F sharp in violas"—"Mutes off gradually."

The orchestra sometimes knows the remark that is coming. The players wait for the reminder at the violas' tune in 'Till Eulenspiegel': "Tune it—the F's always sharp and scratchy!" In the score will probably be found the remark "A word to the violas here! Always shaky!"

The score is never placed nearer to him than the ordinary height of a table, and even in the most unfamiliar work it is noticed that his head is never "in the office", but always erect and facing the orchestra.. He glances at his score, but his eyes are mainly upon the orchestra as a whole or directed at a certain department. Few conductors, if any, help their players so much; whenever possible he looks at the player at the very moment when he needs a lead, his left hand ever ready to emphasize it. He never forgets a bad mistake. If once a department fails at an entry, through a miscount of bar or any other reason, that department may be sure that when next the work is performed the conductor's eye will be upon it like a hawk's. And these particular players will probably have eyes, stick, left hand and the whole of Sir Henry's body focussed upon them, if the original catastrophe was a bad one. Not that he is unkind even after a bad mishap. Only once—after a very sticky part of Beethoven's No. 7—has he conducted a post-mortem next morning when the 1st and 2nd violins were made to play their semiquavers several times by themselves. Usually, whatever the calamity, he takes the attitude—"Well, well, we are all human!" And he grows more human and kindly with the years.

paratively unknown to the orchestra and which have been rushed through only once. When he is on the rostrum, a second or so before starting, his face never shows a worried or anxious mind, though he might well be filled with dismay at the thought of the task before him. His mind is too well trained to admit the word dismay. He commands 100 per cent. of himself, and neither his body nor his mind ever runs to waste. Other men, doing half his work, may tear themselves to pieces, through temperament or other squandering of physical and mental effort. Wood is superbly organized, and every part of him kept in perfect training.

A distinguished fellow-conductor said to him during a Promenade season: "Henry, my dear fellow, I can't understand how you can do these Proms night after night." "No," said Sir Henry; "*you'd* be dead in a fortnight!"

In the last year or two he has not driven himself so hard at rehearsal, but there was a time when he gave almost as much vitality in the mornings as he expended at night, yet seemed to have ample reserves. After he had been seriously ill one spring—his only set-back in health—he instituted a novel form of rehearsal, in which the principal 1st violin took the baton while Wood listened and made his comments in the hall. His opinion always was that it is not possible to hear everything on the rostrum as it sounds in the hall, and he put this scheme into practice for two reasons. It undoubtedly conserved his strength, and at the same time gave him another point of view. The orchestra, however, felt relief when he returned to directing his own rehearsals. One conductor at a time is enough. There is a riddle—"What sounds worse than one viola?" The answer is—"Two!" A reason why Wood's scheme was something of a trial to the players was the fact that the principal violin, then Charles Woodhouse, might rehearse a tempo in 2 beats, and in the evening Sir Henry would possibly take it in 4. And then the actual tempo, in spite of the fact that Woodhouse knew his Sir Henry as well as any one, could never be quite the same. Take for example the opening of the 'Storm' in Beethoven's Pastoral Symphony. C. W. rehearsed this in the morning in 4 beats at a fairly quick tempo. In the evening, from Sir Henry, there came 2 beats only, at a slower tempo. An accident was barely averted. It would have been safer to play the work unrehearsed.

The other reason for the unpopularity of this form of rehearsal was the bringing into operation of the dinner bell's younger brother. This was to save Sir Henry shouting when he wanted to stop. The orchestra will not forget the historic morning when this bell appeared for the first time. It was at one of the first rehearsals on this new scheme, whilst C. W. was running through Debussy's 'L'Après-midi d'un faune'. Sir Henry at the time was invisible, when suddenly, without any warning, the atmosphere was shattered by a violent bell, followed by the emergence of Sir Henry from under the circle, where he had been hiding. For a few moments there was a riot. Sir Henry enjoyed his little joke as much as any. The orchestra never really got used to this bell. Nerves get frayed, and violent bell-ringing becomes trying. The

orchestra used to watch for Wood's hand stealing to his
pocket for the instrument of torture, with something like
dread. Poor C. W. occasionally looked quite numbed after
a protracted period of bell-ringing, for he never could
tell when it was coming. But we could—and held tight.

When this scheme was working Sir Henry left C.W.
on the rostrum and retired to sit in solitary state in the middle
of the first row of the grand circle. There he would
neatly arrange in front of him the miniature score, watch,
glasses, and tea-bell. C. W. would then start on the rehearsal
and conduct under a running commentary from the circle.
Whether Sir Henry remained in his seat or roamed about
at different *tempi* depended upon his reaction to certain
discrepancies in the orchestra. A series of fluffy passages
resulted in his running round the whole circle, followed by
a furious blast of invective. A rehearsal of the 1st movement of Tchaikovsky's Fourth Symphony was fairly
typical of this method. A slight tinkle of the bell brings
to an end the introduction, and the brass are accused of
forcing their tone, and also that the bass is sharp. After
another start Letter C is reached, where the strings, in
their accompanying rhythmic figures, provoke him to ring
the bell again, not so gently, for the wood-wind "does not
get through". "The old story—strings too loud," he
exclaims. "Play one *f*, as it is on paper, not any old thing!
Wind, you must blow out more! Try it again!" Then,
affairs go fairly smoothly until Letter G, when the wood-
wind are found to be playing the semiquavers inaccurately
and therefore blurring their ascending passages. That
rectified, the orchestra, well in its stride, comes to the climax

moderato con anima, but is overwhelmed by a violent cascade from the bell, and Sir Henry's penetrating voice at full power roars:—

"No, no, that's no good, I can't hear anything! At the three *f*'s, strings, play near the bridge and make your tone penetrate. Wood-wind, blow out for all you're worth! And—now you've stopped—strings, the rhythm is not right! When you've got two notes of the same name I never hear the articulation—Letter H, for instance—I don't get the two C sharps—it is fluffy right through the movement. Always the same old story—two notes of the same name do *not* get through unless properly articulated—you needn't force it, but I must hear the two notes! Woodhouse, go on to the coda!" And the movement ends happily, save that the tuba has to play his *crescendo* much stronger in the ascending quavers, four bars before the 1st time bar.

To illustrate the different point of view he obtained, I recall another rehearsal of Beethoven's Eighth Symphony. Wood's comments from the back of the hall are nearly all concerned with balance. Before actually beginning, the orchestra, with the exception of the first and second violins, have orders to be "lenient", and a big *diminuendo* is to be pencilled in the opening bars. The bell preludes his remarks that the 'cellos' reiterated quavers at bar 13 are inaudible, and they must forcibly "ram home" their five notes, otherwise the rhythmic interest is lost. The wind are then told to "shut up instantly on the first beat of the *a tempo* bar, to let through the strings' ascending quavers *pp*, which must not be forced up." A terrific peal from the bell at bar 70 discovers Sir Henry almost stamping up and down the circle, waving his score in the air.

"I don't want any of your cosy *ff*'s—I want a great sound! The utmost power from you! Do it again!" The rest of the movement goes too well for the bell to come into action again—or else there is no time for him to stop. However, considerably more power is demanded at the great moment at bar 190, where he directs in his annotated score that the chromatic timpani crash the whole subject over the devoted heads of the 'cellos, basses and bassoons. The second movement begins with two anticipatory beats to ensure a perfect start—yes, in spite of the vituperation frequently poured upon the heads of those amateur conductors who always give beats for nothing. The first bell goes at bar 23. "I don't hear that black patch—it must be played with the utmost ferocity. I want a tearing *fortissimo*. Don't be afraid of it. You're always so nervous at a black patch because it looks black on paper. Don't be nervous—I'm never nervous! Rip it out and make the old ladies jump!"

A morning's rehearsal for a Promenade concert is very different from that of a normal symphony concert. To begin with, there are pieces from three or four programmes, and the covers, at the preliminary rehearsal, are as thick as two family bibles, for there are some thirty pieces a day to work through. Before the first concert Wood now has eight full rehearsals. All the new music will be run through once, and also the less familiar works such as Sibelius's symphonies. But apart from some particular compositions in the usual repertory that are singled out, Wood will generally play piece after piece straight through, particularly those in the early part of the season. A few years ago he took one or two works like Dukas's 'Apprenti-Sorcier', or Bantock's 'Pierrot of the Minute' and played them over and over again at these rehearsals. Recently, however, he does little intensive rehearsing before the season, using the time for a comprehensive survey of as many works as possible.

On the Saturday morning before the first night he usually takes the opportunity of saying: "No carelessness! We are rehearsing now. I want riveted attention. Don't make me stop for nothing—I've got a lot to get through. We've not done any real rehearsing yet, you know!" The players sigh, thinking of all the slogging they have already been through. On a morning untroubled by composers Wood usually tackles the programme for the same evening, playing it all if he can. If there is a difficult work down for the next day he may rough it out, but rather than spend much time on a particular piece he will make sure of the classics and all familiar works. Rarely will he play a symphony or a tone-poem unrehearsed, whatever demands are made by new works. In the 1936 season, Tchaikovsky's Pathetic Symphony was the only big piece in the entire programme which was played absolutely unrehearsed. Haydn's and Mozart's symphonies are never left to chance, whatever happens. A Haydn symphony is far more difficult than a modern one. "It shows—it shows!" is a favourite remark of Wood's.

At a rehearsal for a Bach concert he almost always announces that he will do all the "other stuff" first, and keep only those players concerned in the Bach programme from 11.0 a.m. onwards. On a Saturday morning he often runs through the orchestral part only of a big Wagner extract, and so it goes on. One or two works ahead, if possible, and always a "safety first" run-through for the evening's concert. The concerto is timed for about 12.20, and the arias at 12.45 p.m., according to the length of the pieces. The doubtful factor of Sir Henry's scheming is, I have said, the composer-conductor. Wherever possible he encourages the composer to conduct his own work, for it saves him strain and also gives him a sound idea of the composer's *tempi*, if he himself is performing it later. He sits in the circle with a score and makes notes of the composer's comments, and if an inexperienced conductor is having difficulty he will freely make helpful suggestions. "I should beat that in 6, it is clearer for the orchestra!" "Tell the brass to make that passage *piano*—you'll find it's all right then!"

Some composers have little idea of time when rehearsing. They become absorbed in their music and forget that, during the Promenade season especially, a time-table is important. A distinguished composer, at the beginning of the season, apologized to the orchestra for the amount of time he was taking to rehearse, and a voice from the clarinet department was heard to mutter: "It's all right! Tell him we've got another eight weeks!"

There is sometimes a happy moment when a conductor, seeking advice from the rostrum, peers into the dimness of the hall, to find Sir Henry gone from the seat in which he last saw him. "It's all right, I'm here," comes a voice from quite another position, like the Cheshire Cat's. When

Dame Ethel Smyth was rehearsing one of her pieces, Wood had seated himself with the score in the circle just over the first violins. After a stop she suddenly turned to him with a question.

"Henry, I can't hear the horn, can you?" But his seat is empty.

"Drat the man! He's gone. Henry—Hen . . . ry! Where are you?"

Somewhere a voice from the darkness in another part of the hall: "No, he wasn't playing—do it again. And now you've stopped, I should mark your trombones down a bit —they're too heavy."

Dame Ethel searches for a pencil, unsuccessfully. Again comes a voice from the void: "You'll find a pencil on the stand."

Later on the pencil again eludes her, and another search takes place. "What's the matter now?" says the voice. "Lost your handkerchief?" Applause from the orchestra.

Wood often takes as much interest in these works as the composers themselves. He will shout, while the orchestra is still playing, "That passage is fluffy! I should try it again; the strings are hurrying!" One thing he will not tolerate—bad parts. Woe to the composer who has in-accuracies in his orchestral parts! He has been known to say in his wrath: "Take it away and get it corrected by to-morrow—I can't waste time now!" He then mounts the rostrum again, and while taking off his coat, mutters —"These composers! Why don't they look after their music as I do? They should run through every note—you can't trust copyists—wasting my time! They think their work is everything—what about my symphony? and the overture and the concerto and the arias? That doesn't matter, of course!... Now, come on, we've wasted enough time already.... Leonora No. 3.... Observe that *diminuendo* in the third bar—it's no good starting it too softly! And the utmost ferocity on that first chord! No, no, that's no good. I can't hear it, and your open G is too sharp, strings. Again! Play what you've got on paper!"

Except in the coldest weather he works in a waistcoat, with pencils sticking out of each pocket. Completely efficient, he loses no moment in searching for anything, while his eye is ever moving over the orchestra to see what the back desks are doing. He is quick to notice any discrepancy in bowing of the strings. His ear is one of the finest, and bad intonation is quickly trounced. He has tried every method of tuning. For years, every member of the orchestra, save the basses and kitchen department, were ordered to parade in the artists' room before the concert, not only to ensure that everyone was present but also to take the two A's (one wind, one strings) from a home-made barrel-organ which, placed just to the left of the door as one went in, was churned by a rather gloomy-looking man. For half an hour a ceaseless procession of instrumentalists filed past this contraption and tuned their instruments while Wood sat alertly cheerful in his arm-chair. He would take a good look at each instrument, and say "Too sharp!" or "Too flat!"—generally the former. He looked carefully each time, because on one occasion a certain string department ("trying it on") brought in the same instrument fourteen times. After that he was wary. The man has no "nerves" at all in the temperamental sense. What other conductor could listen to this A-droning for 30 minutes before a concert, without going berserk? Yet he, seated in his chair, never seemed to mind it for a moment.

Things that drive an average musician to exasperation do not appear to touch him at all. When Queen's Hall was redecorated in "elephant's breath", all his preliminary rehearsals were accompanied by incessant hammering. Loud hammering; not just tapping. Then came bands of men laying carpets and dropping things; also groups of mechanics fitting up chairs; and lastly the sucking noise of a new kind of vacuum-cleaner broke out at odd times. (After the concerts started the extrinsic noise came mainly from the ventilating-plant.) Just hammering, sometimes loud and sometimes weak; but breaking out like a plague of wood-peckers; one moment from behind the organ, the next from the opposite end of the hall. If the attendant rushed to the place where the hammering was taking place he would be too late and it would be heard in another part of the hall. Yet with all this distraction Wood only rarely seemed to be upset. Occasionally he would put his coat on and leave the platform for a moment or two and send for the manager, but most of the time he ignored the noises—except when the hammering rhythm just didn't coincide with that of the piece. Incredible as this may sound, all this went on throughout the season, and yet he completed his huge task as easily as if Queen's Hall were normal, with nothing but its draughts to annoy. The nerves of the orchestral players frayed before Sir Henry's did.

At times he seems to be superhuman, so utterly absent

in him are the ordinary temperamental weaknesses of most artists. His constitution is like iron, his mind clear and concentrated, and his temperament predominantly cheerful. He may become heated if, because of subdued conversation, he cannot make himself heard. "Chatter, chatter, chatter! This is a rehearsal, not a mothers' meeting! Work in silence! How can I hear anything if you talk? Keep silence!" He is completely indifferent to what the audience or critics may say or think. He feels the music he is interpreting in a certain way, and that is the end of it all. People may like or not like his ideas, but, "That's their funeral; I know what *I* feel about it," says Sir Henry. He performs all his work with perfect sincerity and intense interest.

A vital part of his equipment is his control and understanding of his players. There are never any incidents. At times, some years ago, he may have driven some of his orchestra near to breaking point—by his bell, or perpetual repetition, or incessant demands for "More sound—I want the utmost ferocity. It's far too namby-pamby." Then, when every one is weary: "Now turn back to the beginning, we'll play it all through once more!" But he always senses the danger-point, beyond which he does not go. Particularly in later years this understanding has been more fully shown to the orchestra. His whole personality, always immensely vital and kindly, has grown mellow, and whereas in the past he became exasperated over a moment's carelessness or false intonation, smiles are now more frequent, and he does not hold forth over "the carelessness of a professional orchestra." In spite of grumbles at endless rehearsals, and much heart-breaking repetition and striving, the orchestra has always paid him deep respect and his every demand has been met with loyalty. Sir Henry, pioneer of first-rate orchestral playing in this country, has not only steadily laboured to raise the status of the orchestral player, but has succeeded. He takes a special interest in those players who have been through his training. If they are called upon as soloists or as composers or are in any way singled out for a special piece of work, he will give them his special help and advice and that little extra time in rehearsal which may make a vital difference. He puts himself to any amount of trouble to make this venture a success, whatever demands are being made of him at the time. In the same way he will write personal letters. Nothing is too much trouble, and nothing that should be done by himself is delegated. When the Queen's Hall Orchestra used to play at Promenade concerts, Saturday afternoon symphony concerts, and double Sunday concerts, it was very much Sir Henry's personal affair. No other conductor used to perform with it, and no deputies whatever were allowed. Before the B.B.C. took over, this was the only orchestra outside the "deputy system." Every player who wished to join the orchestra played in audition to him at Queen's Hall—and a cold, miserable undertaking it was, with the hall half dark and completely empty. Then Sir Henry sat by himself hour after hour, listening to prospective orchestral players, and would-be soloists as well. "Thank you very much for playing to me. Good morning." Mysterious changes in the personnel used to take place, year after year. Faces would disappear and new ones come, but nobody beside

Sir Henry and Robert Newman would know the why and wherefore. But once a player in a key position made good, it was rare that he left unless of his own accord.

Wood never gives anything away. He used to say, "When I have my eye on a certain player who is fooling about, I look the other way to make him feel secure—but I'm watching him all right!" His eyes are piercing, and they are frequently seen to rove, intensely alive to every movement of the orchestra. He hates all unnecessary movement on the platform, since it not only distracts the audience, but also himself; and here is another instance of his thoroughness and wealth of experience. When he has noted in certain pieces that the turning of pages disturbs a very quiet moment in the music, he either has another turn arranged by the copyist, or else, if there is time, writes in blue pencil across the page—"Don't turn until the pianist begins the *forte*" (as in the Emperor concerto).

He has special parts for the overture of 'Tannhäuser', for instance, so that the violins in their celebrated figure accompanying the Pilgrims' March in 3/4 time, should not suddenly lose power when half their number have to turn. He pasted two pages on top of each other, so that forty lines can be read without turning. It means that enormously high covers appear on the stands for this piece, as tall as newspapers; but there is no disturbance, and the vital power is sustained throughout. He was so irritated by the dropping of mutes that he provided all the string players with a special spring-clip mute, which clipped on to the stands. This certainly lessened the droppings, though they were not very good mutes. One can take it that every invention for the efficiency of the orchestra has been tried by him, and only abandoned when found wanting.

He has experimented with every seating plan, and nowadays has his first and second violins together, 'celli opposite them at his right hand, and spreading out in a semi-circle around him in front, and immediately behind them, on the first rise, the violas, with the basses as near as possible to the 'celli. First flute is on the right of the first line of wood-wind, first clarinet immediately behind him, and first horn behind the clarinet. First oboe and bassoon sit in the middle, on the right of their departments. His chief idea, in the strings, is that generally the first and second violins are playing similar parts as are the 'celli and basses, especially in the classics, so that his arrangement makes matters of ensemble easier. Ensemble and intonation have ever been his chief cares, and no conductor in this country has done more to inculcate an ideal into our orchestras. As an orchestra trainer Wood is indefatigable, as in all things else, and it is doubtful whether our orchestras, which are now able to hold their own with the best of Europe, could have reached this position without his influence.

His incessant maintenance of the standard is kept up through the strain of a Promenade season, as in any performance in which he is engaged. Sparing no one, and himself least of all, he extracts every ounce of vitality. He has a partiality for big things in all musical matters. "I want a great volume of sound!" Always he likes as large an orchestra as possible; as he says, it is good for employment. He hates anything tinkling and small—harpsichord tone, for instance—and although critics may denounce his highly-coloured scoring of Handel and Bach, the public adores it, and it is always interesting for the orchestra. A feature of his scoring is the exploitation of all his instruments. It is refreshing for his violas to be allowed to play in their upper positions in Handel.

Free from all inhibitions, Wood makes music as he finds it, refusing to be trammelled in any way by what others think—supremely confident of himself. He carries the orchestra with him with the greatest ease, driving as hard as he can, but just with safety. Such a life must be lived always in strict training, like an athlete's. During the Promenade season he obeys a rigorous routine, interrupted only by a rest on Sundays. Starting work frequently before breakfast, he is at Queen's Hall at 9.45 a.m. and rehearses until 1.0 p.m. Then he takes a piano rehearsal with next day's soloists, sometimes not leaving Queen's Hall until 2.30 p.m. After lunch, more work on scores until 4.30, when he is invariably massaged. At 5.30 he has some light food and goes to bed for an hour, getting up again in time to dress for Queen's Hall, where he always used to arrive at 7.30. Now that he no longer supervises the tuning, he arrives at 7.45 p.m.

Few people realize that during the last two or three weeks of the Promenade concerts Wood conducts the R.A.M. Orchestra on two afternoons in the week. Immediately after the Promenade season he takes charge of concerts all over the provinces.

He has been singularly endowed with gifts apart from music. As a landscape painter he would probably have attained as distinguished a position as he now holds in music, had he chosen to devote himself wholly to that path. He is no mere amateur, even though he only works now at holiday times. He is also extremely efficient with his hands in the rougher arts of carpentry and carving. Master of his mind in his concentration, he is no less its master in relaxation.

Sir Henry Wood is one of the great men of England's long musical history.